PADDY STRONGE

SUCCESSFUL

INVESTING

HOW TO MAKE MONEY
IN THE STOCK MARKET

FROM REAL LIFE EXPERIENCE

Contents

Dedication

To my wife Eleanor

A wondrous life shared for over fifty years.

Acknowledgments

I want to put on record my thanks to Ellen Kane, our illustrator, who did the Cartoons of me with my Greyhound Duff, for this Book. She succeeded admirably in creating a touch of humour at the start of each chapter.

I must also thank all those who supported me when writing this Book. Foremost is all my family. They ensured that when I relied on logic, my arguments were well founded and clearly expressed. I must mention my daughter Clare who was ever present giving me advice and writing the Introduction to the Book. I must also mention my twin brother Bill who added value to my deliberations. As he has lived in the US for many years he was helpful in looking at things from the perspective of a US investor.

I was delighted that my eldest grandchild Adam brought me the perspective of the "social media" generation!

There were also a couple of golfing buddies from my own generation, who read the Book and made some helpful suggestions. While I readily agree that I don't get many birdies on the course, I am hoping that I do a little better off the course!

Finally, I would like to thank those that made the effort to read the Book and endorsed it. Their endorsements will encourage a wider readership of the Book. Thanks guys!

Endorsements

Conor O'Donoghue

"This book gives a comprehensive review of an investment journey through thick and thin. New and experienced stock market participants will find much to enjoy with lots of learnings for the uninitiated and practical tips for the more seasoned investor."

Conor O'Donoghue is an adviser on pensions and investments. He has previously worked for Merrill Lynch in the US and more recently for Davy stockbrokers in Ireland.

Rupert Rhodd

"This Book uses readily available internet sources to establish the soundness of individual companies. The book is a very useful guide for US investors who wish to add overseas stocks to ensure a more diversified portfolio."

Rupert Rhodd is Economics Professor & Associate Dean of the College of Business at Florida Atlantic University, U.S.A. He received his PhD from Fordham University New York.

Nick Hewer

"In times of economic turmoil, when stocks are haemorrhaging, following some simple rules, an ordinary small-time investor can profit handsomely. This book is an everyday companion particularly for the occasional investor who likes a challenge but wants to know how to maximize the return whilst minimizing the risk."

Nick Hewer is a retired UK television presenter, company director and former public relations consultant. From 2005 to 2014, he appeared as Alan Sugar's adviser in the British television series The Apprentice. From 2012 to 2021, he presented the Channel 4 program Countdown.

Jim Power

"This book provides a wealth of information on the principles of investment; historical events and most importantly the lessons learned from personal experience. It is written in a jargon-free way and at the same time explains the jargon that permeates the markets. All readers will find it a worthwhile read and people of all levels of experience will take something from it."

Jim Power has a wealth of experience in delivering insightful economic analysis, forecasts and commentary to both Irish and international audiences. He writes regularly for national newspapers and is a regular contributor to radio and TV debates and discussions, and podcasts such as The Stand and Win Happy.

About the Author

Paddy Stronge is an experienced banker in Ireland, the UK, and the USA. He was Chief Operating Officer at Bank of Ireland Corporate Banking. He has consulted for clients in Central and Eastern Europe, Russia, and selected Asian/Caribbean/South American countries. He is an economics graduate from University College Dublin and became a Fellow of both the Chartered Association of Certified Accountants and the Irish Institute of Bankers.

Paddy has lectured on Finance and Investment at undergraduate and graduate levels in leading universities and professional Institutes in Ireland and abroad. He is the executive chairman of e-commerce company Philos IT. He lives in Dublin with his wife Eleanor and his rescue greyhound Duff.

Together with his grandson Adam, Paddy runs an investing and market analysis video podcast called **The Investment Hound**. For the latest stock market tips and investing insights, follow **The Investment Hound** on Instagram and TikTok or listen to **The Investment Hound** podcast on Spotify, Apple Podcasts, and all other podcast platforms.

Introduction

"This is my favourite kind of drama"

There is a moment every morning on business TV channels when the markets open for that day's trading.

A breathlessly excited news anchor stands in front of a gigantic wall with the biggest stocks listed in small black squares behind.

Then, in a split second, as the markets open, the entire wall lights up, with each square turning green or red depending if the stock is up or down on the previous day's closing price.

It is the precise moment that simultaneously attracts and repels people from owning shares and becoming involved in the stock market.

For those that enjoy investing, this is the moment when you can see how overnight trading in Asia or America has impacted the price of your shares (if you're based in Europe). It is the latest twist or turn in the exciting story of owning investments in the stock market.

For others, however, this enormous wall, full of strange acronyms such as S&P and FTSE and categories of shares such as Banks, Automobiles, and Technology, not to mention an endless stream of ticker-tape text across the bottom of the screen showing the rise and fall of stock after stock, is overwhelming, confusing, and jeopardous.

Yet, despite this unnerving impression, the long-term evidence shows that the stock market is one of the safest and most lucrative places to invest your money.

If you look at stock market returns since the 1920s, individuals have very rarely lost money buying shares and holding them for a 20-year period in that time.

Even considering market disasters such as the Great Depression, World War II, Black Monday, the Tech Bubble of the early 2000s, and of course, the Global Financial Crisis, investors would have experienced significant gains had they made an investment in the S&P 500 (in New York) and held it uninterrupted for 20 years.

Of course, there are clearly ups and downs along the way.

It's not unusual for stocks to drop 10% or 20% in value over a short period of time, but generally, most stocks will bounce back from these temporary dips, often within a year.

<u>And the overall trend across all markets is usually up.</u>

And did I mention Dividends?

A Dividend is a portion of the profits that companies pay out to their shareholders (usually quarterly, half-yearly, or annually).

It is a cash amount deposited into your account by a company for simply owning a share of their business. It is used by the company as a reward for new investors and to entice existing investors to stick around.

To make money in the short and long term in the stock market, the key is to buy shares that pay out good Dividends and hold them for years rather than weeks or months.

If you follow this approach, you will earn an income each year from your Dividends while, over the long term, the value of most of your shares is increasing.

So, if it's that simple, what goes wrong?

Why isn't everyone invested in the stock market and making lots of money?

My experience is that inexperienced investors make the same mistakes over and over again. They think emotionally, relying on gut feelings rather than examining the facts.

They buy because someone tells them they have just made money on a rising share price. They follow the tip and invest in the share when the price has already risen.

These same investors then sell because someone tells them the share price has fallen, and they should quickly get out. In short, they follow a foolproof technique for losing money: Buy high and sell low.

Not a good idea!

In this book, I would like to demystify the stock market and empower amateur investors, battle-scarred investors, young people, mid-lifers, and pensioners to consider the stock market as a safe way to both save for the future and generate income.

To do this, I will explain the basics of how the stock market works and how to invest in individual shares in a safe and smart way.

I'll introduce technical insight on how to time your purchase of a share most effectively. I'll explain the key signals that indicate an individual share is underperforming and should be sold.

And importantly, I will go through a list of easy risk management techniques you can use to protect your money once you are invested.

I will also take the reader on a personal story through the ups and downs of my own stock market portfolio, which began in the ashes of the global financial crisis of 2008 and went on to weather the rollercoaster years in the market of the Covid-19 pandemic and the outbreak of war in Ukraine.

I began as a previously infrequent investor in the stock market to build a stock portfolio just as the disastrous consequences of the subprime mortgage crisis in 2007 were beginning to unfold around the world.

From this dramatic beginning, over a number of years, I invested almost €200,000 in the stock market in the following sectors: Banks, Oil & Basic Resources, Automobiles, Pharmaceuticals, Utilities, UK Retail, Insurance, Telecoms, Property & Construction, and a variety of US, UK, German and Irish companies.

Just before Covid-19 hit in February 2020, I had Realized (in cash) Gains of €32,731 and Unrealized Gains (not yet in cash) of €41,785, totaling a little under €75,000 in capital gains.

Plus, I had generated an annual income going forward of c.€11,000 from Dividends.

The average Dividend yield on the portfolio was 5.76% per annum. Compare that to the 0.1% interest I would have earned by putting my money 'safely in the bank'.

In total, I had made in excess of €150,000 over the period from 2008 to early 2020. *A good return from an investment building up over the years to almost €200,000.*

It was clear that people who were afraid to buy shares in the aftermath of the Financial Crisis had lost out badly.

However, in March 2020, the markets experienced another major upheaval as the novel Coronavirus Covid-19 began to spread rapidly around the world, bringing life as we knew it to a standstill.

The market shock from Covid-19 was catastrophic for my investments: In one month, <u>my portfolio suffered a loss in valuations of €100,000+.</u>

Tentatively, and I emphasize tentatively, I used the lessons I learned from the aftermath of the financial crisis to carry out a restructure of my portfolio.

Happily, I can report that fifteen months later, the portfolio had fully recovered from the Covid-19 shock, with valuations back to their pre-Covid peak of February 2020.

In fact, by December 2021, the portfolio was a further €30,000+ ahead of its pre-Covid high.

And then…on the morning of 24th February 2022, Putin sent his forces into Ukraine, and the market was thrown into chaos by yet another major global event: war in Europe.

Markets suffered a shock around the world, with the DAX in Frankfurt particularly affected, reflecting German reliance on Russian energy supplies. Yet, within weeks, markets had fully recovered their losses.

However, in addition to war at the edges of Europe, global markets are currently also facing record inflation and rising interest rates.

As the reader will quickly see, global events impact the stock market, and you will need to hold your nerve. But what is most important is to remember that market crashes also create opportunities.

Buy into well-known companies that pay attractive dividends when market prices are at a low ebb.

In this book, I will share the lessons I learned navigating the stock market through these financial, pandemic, and wartime global disruptions.

It is my hope that my simple explanations for how the stock market works combined with stories of my real-world experience investing through these turbulent times will provide a solid foundation – as well as a real insight into what works and doesn't work - for each investor as they undertake their own stock market journey.

Happy reading and enjoy the ride!

Section A

Building a Share Portfolio:
A Real-Life Story

This section of the book deals with the stock market journey that I personally undertook, building a portfolio of shares from nothing.

It began just after the Global Financial Crisis, which had adversely impacted the stock market in 2008/9, and concluded at a pre-pandemic position in February 2020.

In Section B, I will show you how the portfolio was affected by the arrival of Covid-19, the effect of the pandemic on the portfolio, and the ups and downs in the subsequent months and years right up to the invasion of Ukraine.

In Section C, the final section of the Book, I will talk about investment strategies and risk management and provide an easy 10-step checklist that you can use to assess any company's share when you are considering a purchase.

Starting off, building a share portfolio was a personal learning experience as I had been, up till then, an occasional investor. I was now learning through my successes and failures how to do things correctly.

Looking back, I am surprised that I was overall quite successful, and I think that the following observations may help to explain matters:

In most instances, I limited the size of each holding to €5,000.

Taking this bitesize approach ensured that any subsequent losses were relatively small. Of course, the subsequent profits were less too.

But the approach of small-size investments also naturally encouraged me to diversify my holdings, spreading my investments across a lot of companies, sectors, and countries.

As I will deal with later in the book, diversification is a key approach to ensuring that risks are spread, with the expectation that – overall – losses in some holdings can be offset by profits elsewhere.

As a retired pensioner, I was able to devote time and effort to managing my shares. I enjoy dealing in shares, and for me, the activity is another hobby to enjoy.

I hope you will find the insights learned from building my portfolio useful, and you, yourself, might even undertake a similarly enjoyable journey.

Chapter One

At the Beginning:

The Financial Crisis of 2007 – 2008

Let's start at the start.

What is a share?

Shares are units of ownership of a company, usually traded on the stock market. They are also known as stocks or equities.

A share can be issued by a company that is listed on a stock market.

Well-known stock markets include the New York Stock Exchange, the London Stock Exchange, the Tokyo Stock Exchange, and the Frankfurt Stock Exchange. I invested in all these stock exchanges.

On these stock markets, the top performing companies are often grouped together into what is called an 'index'.

The Standard and Poor's 500 (S&P 500) index tracks the performance of the 500 largest companies in several US stock markets.

The FTSE 100 index follows the fortunes of the 100 largest companies on the London Stock Exchange. The Nikkei index in Tokyo tracks a weighted average of the 225 top Japanese companies, and in Germany, the DAX index tracks the 40 biggest companies listed on the Frankfurt Stock Exchange.

We tend to talk about the Index rather than the stock market as it gives you a clearer picture of the health of the most important companies in a market.

Why does a company's share price go up or down?

Individual share prices usually increase in value because

companies reinvest some of their profits back into the business each year.

This reinvestment allows the company to expand and grow the business, which should generate even bigger profits in the future.

These higher earnings will usually propel increases in the company's share price.

On the other hand, if, either through mismanagement or misfortune, a company's profits start to fall, then the share price usually falls too.

Investors try to be ahead of the game. They buy the share now, expecting that, as the company's fortunes improve, they will make a profit.

They follow the one golden rule of investing:

You never invest in the past; you invest in the future.

My investment portfolio began at an all-time low in the global stock markets, from where the future looked very uncertain: the Financial Crash of 2007-2008.

What caused the Financial Crash?

As the 2000s unfolded, there was almost a decade of steady economic growth.

In many Developed Economies, easy and cheap mortgages became readily available, leading to higher and higher house prices.

The average house price in the UK skyrocketed from £100,000 in 2000 to just under £225,000 in 2007.

In the US, 'subprime' mortgages - or portion of mortgages where the risk of failure to repay was high - were repackaged and given good ratings by Ratings Agencies (such as Standard & Poor's and Moody's).

They were then sold globally, implicating very many countries worldwide in the disastrous consequences of these bad loans.

As the volume and reach of these bad loans came to light, a light was similarly shone on poor mortgage lending practices in other countries.

The international financial system was nearly destroyed due to the failure (or near failure) of several major banks, mortgage lenders, and insurance companies.

This banking catastrophe led to the worst economic downturn since the Great Depression of 1929 – 1939.

All major stock markets across the world declined sharply.

The S&P 500 fell 52% between 5th April 2007 and 2nd February 2009.

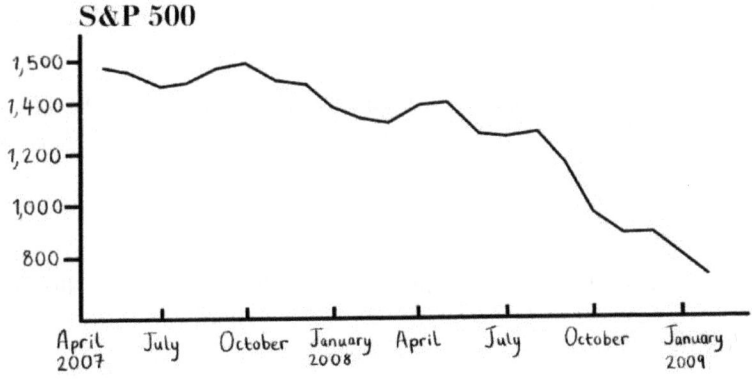

The **DAX** also fell by 52% around the same time:

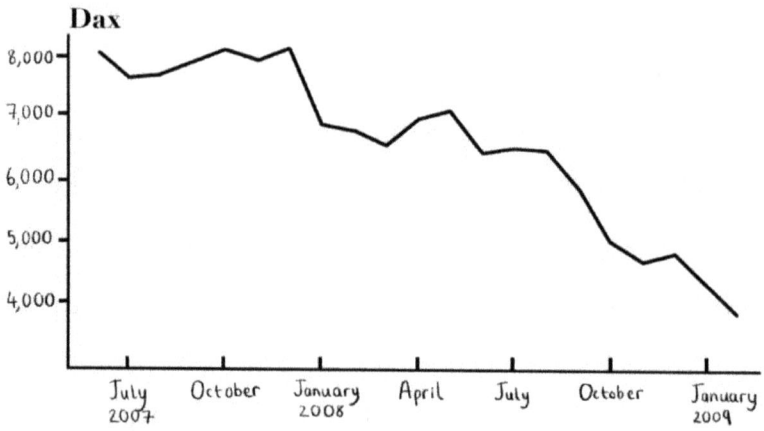

The **FTSE 100** declined by 43% from a pre-financial crisis peak to a post-financial crisis low:

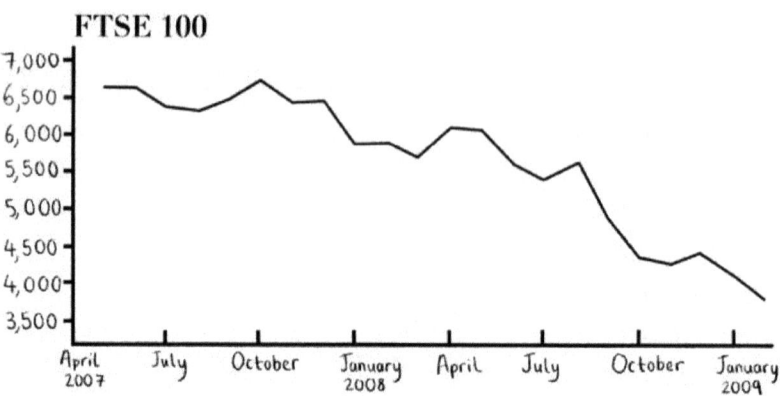

Stock prices were slaughtered in all markets. No investor escaped.

Nowhere was this worse than for those who held bank shares.

This is because the health of banks mirrors the health of the economy. If the economy tanks, bank shares will tank due to high Bad Debts.

Look at what happened to this Index, which tracks the performance of Europe's top 600 banks:

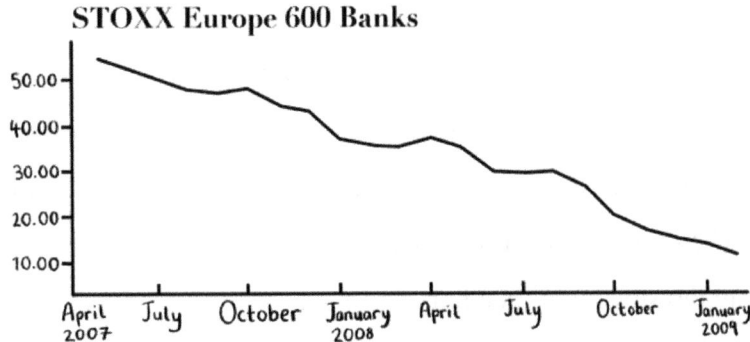

Many investors who were invested in Irish bank shares suffered almost a complete wipe-out.

Most bank shareholders and there were very many of them, were 'caught in the headlights' watching the obliteration of their 'safe and secure' bank shares.

They failed to react. They (including me) should have sold their shares when it became clear that the share prices of Irish banks were falling much further than the global average drop of 40-50%.

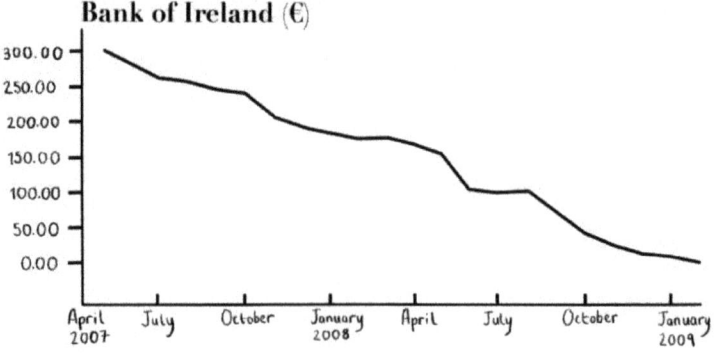

We couldn't believe what was happening!

Many savers - to this day - are scarred by their experience holding shares during the Financial Crash of 2007 – 2009. They are too afraid that they will lose money if they invest in the stock market again.

But let's look at how the markets performed <u>after</u> the crash of 2007 and 2008.

The S&P 500 more than tripled in value.

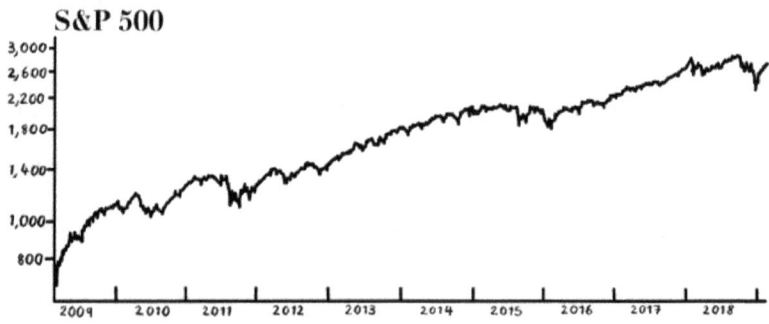

The FTSE 100 delivered average *annual* returns of 10.75% in the period 2009 - 2017. Similarly, the DAX delivered slightly under 13% average annual growth between January 2009 and January 2020.

The irony for these scarred investors is that the Global Financial Crisis was an enormous investing opportunity.

Why? What goes down must come up!

When the stock market drops sharply because of a crisis, share prices will usually normalize and return to growth (in time).

It is when circumstances in the market are <u>at their worst</u> that opportunities are most ripe for investors.

Contrarian investing - doing what others are afraid to do - is often the most successful approach when it comes to maximizing returns.

Baron Rothschild, an 18th-century member of the Rothschild banking family, is credited with saying:

"The time to buy is when there's blood in the streets."

He should know.

Rothschild made a fortune buying in the panic that followed the Battle of Waterloo defeat for Napoleon.

But that's not the whole story.

The original quote is believed to be:

"Buy when there's blood in the streets, even if the blood is your own."

A great time to invest is when the markets have suffered significant declines.

This is **especially important** if your own portfolio has suffered a significant hit from the crash.

You can pick up 'bargains' to offset any losses as the value of newly purchased shares goes up as the markets return to normal.

Don't be afraid to get involved when the markets have just suffered a significant crash.

Chapter Two

Blood in the Streets: Bank Shares

"Sure.. the safest place for your money
is the bank"

In 2008, there was definitely "blood in the streets," including my own.

It was now time to enter the fray and buy shares, betting that they would 'bounce back' from their all-time lows. I started with the sector I know best from my own career in banking.

Bank shares...are you serious! John McEnroe, tennis star (misquoted)

The US dollar was very weak in 2008 when €1 could buy, at its peak, $1.599, so dollar shares were cheap in euro terms.

I decided to look Stateside for lowly priced bank shares that would be even more valuable by purchasing them with a strong euro.

Another reason I looked at American banks was that, even though the subprime mortgage crisis was 'created' in the US, the bad loans were mostly sold *outside* the US with the result that, ironically, American banks were <u>less exposed</u> to these bad debts.

As a result, I reckoned that US banks should recover faster than some of the other major international banks from this crisis.

Wells Fargo

Wells Fargo was the third largest bank in the U.S. by total assets.

Too big to be allowed to fail!

The purchase of Wells Fargo shares at such a low dollar exchange rate was compelling.

In 2008, I bought 147 Wells Fargo bank shares at $25 each and an all-in cost, including transaction charges, of €3,754... a modest (first) foray into the 'cauldron.'

How did the Wells Fargo share price perform since the purchase?

Very well, indeed!

I then decided to sell 50 shares in 2015 to lock in €1,226 in profits, but I held on to 97 shares to keep a shareholding in the bank.

But then, problems started to occur in Wells Fargo...

US Federal regulators reveal Wells Fargo employees secretly created millions of unauthorized bank and credit card accounts without their customers knowing it. Wells Fargo paid its employees bonuses based on the number of these new accounts they created. Subsequently, account charges were levied on the customers.

The bank was hit with a $185 million fine.

Problem solved? Not really...see next!

Later on, Wells Fargo was accused of modifying mortgages without authorization from their customers. Some customers could have ended up paying the bank more than they owed.... *and...*

The bank admitted it charged at least 570,000 customers *(yeah, over half a million)* for auto insurance they did not need."

Wells Fargo then said in an internal review that approximately 20,000 customers may have defaulted on their car loans for related reasons.

... and then even worse ...

The US Federal Reserve announced that it had prohibited further growth by Wells Fargo until the firm improved its governance and controls.

I was worried: Should I get the hell out?

The Dollar exchange rate had moved strongly in my favor as the value of a Euro fell from $1.50 to $1.20.

The stronger dollar encouraged a sale.

The remaining shares were sold in March 2018, accumulating **net gains of €3,229 from the two Wells**

Fargo sales, with almost 1/4 of the gain due to the strengthening US dollar.

Overall, the capital gains were 85% of the purchase cost.

Cash in your profits and sell when dark clouds appear on the horizon!

Back to 2008...

I decided to do some 'bottom fishing' in the shares of the Irish Banks...maybe claw back a little of the very significant losses that I had incurred on Irish bank shares held during the Financial Crash.

Permanent TSB Holdings (PTSB)

PTSB is a provider of personal financial services in Ireland.

A small holding of PTSB shares was purchased in 2008 as the Bank had a well-regarded Life & Pensions Insurance subsidiary, and very importantly, the bank had negligible exposure to property developers!

During the following year, it became apparent that, with the continuing declines in <u>Residential Property</u> prices, PTSB would suffer enormous losses on their residential mortgages.

The share price had ticked up ever so slightly, and in August 2009, the shares were sold, suffering a miniscule loss of -€24 arising from transaction charges associated with the sale.

No great harm was done, and in retrospect, a very wise move...

Maybe it was time to try the bigger Irish Banks instead.

AIB

AIB (Allied Irish Banks plc) was one of the major banks in Ireland.

AIB offers personal, business, and corporate banking services.

In August 2009, 1,000 shares were bought in AIB at an all-in cost of €2,143...a modest but very daring purchase!

And then manna from heaven...

Sep 17, 2009: The Irish Independent reported that investors in New York believed that the setting up of a Bad Bank (NAMA) by the Irish Government to take over all Property Developers' loans from the Irish Banks would be good for shareholders and the banks.

These US investors voted with their wallets, buying AIB shares and (briefly) sending the price up by 60% from €2.075 to €3.32 per share.

I moved fast and sold the AIB shares in September 2009, making a profit of €1,153.

Strike while the iron is hot!

Bank of Ireland

Bank of Ireland Group is another of the major Irish banks.

The Bank operated in every corner of Irish commercial life and had extensive operations in the UK.

Bank of Ireland was my alma mater, and I refused to believe things were as bad as I feared.

Whaaaaat……I hear you cry!!

I was hoping for a bargain, and so I purchased small lots of Bank of Ireland shares in 2009 and again in early 2010.

I also took up my 'rights' entitlements in 2010 and 2011, adding to my holdings. A 'rights' entitlement is when large discounts are offered by the bank to existing shareholders to entice them to buy new shares.

I then noticed, at the end of 2013, that the Bank of Ireland Price to Book ratio was trading at 1.5 times.

This was equivalent to pre-crisis norms.

What is the Price/Book?

The Price-to-Book ratio (P/B Ratio) is important for anyone interested in investing in bank shares.

It is a ratio used to compare a share's current value to its 'book' value.

The book value is how much the assets (mainly loans) of a bank are worth based on what they cost the bank (the cost price). The market value is how much those same loans can be sold for today, i.e., current valuations.

Before the financial crisis, most bank shares were valued at c. 1.5 times the 'book' value, i.e., they were considered to be more valuable because it was expected that, over time, customers would pay back <u>more</u> to the banks than what the banks had lent them (i.e., through interest and fees).

In 2013 Bank of Ireland's P/B ratio had returned to pre-crisis norms, and I realized there was no reason why bank loans would be more profitable post-crisis than they were pre-crisis, especially given the financial pressures that loan borrowers were experiencing as the crisis unfolded.

I sold the Bank of Ireland shares at a price of €8 per share, making capital gains from the sales of €2,316.

Was the sale of the Bank of Ireland shares at that time a good idea?

You betcha!

By December 2019, the share price was trading at a significantly lower €4.88…*a bullet dodged!*

Mind you, I could have made bigger profits if I had sold <u>a little</u> later.

But you never lose money when you sell at a profit.

What other bank shares are likely to recover well when the Financial Crash starts to recede?

Northern Europe is the richer part of the EU. Maybe bank shares in these countries would prove profitable as these wealthy economies strengthen post-crash.

ING Bank

ING Bank is a Dutch Bank. It is a global financial institution with a strong European base and with more than 51,000 employees who offer retail and wholesale banking services to customers in over 40 countries.

The ING share price had not made a sustained or significant recovery since its dramatic fall in 2008.

The relatively low price for a highly reputable Dutch bank was very tempting.

In 2011, I saw that the price had recently declined from a temporary high to €5.81.

In August 2011, I purchased 589 ING shares at an all-in cost of €3,424.

How did the share price perform since the purchase?

The share price rose steadily, and I sold the ING holding in November 2013 at €9.66 per share, realizing gains of €2,051.

You can get a lot more than tulips from Amsterdam!

Buying unloved ING bank shares, which operated in a big and strong economy, proved to be a smart move.

How about more Bank shares from the US of A?

JP Morgan Chase is a leading global financial services firm with assets of $2.5 trillion and a presence in over 100 markets.

They have over 250,000 employees and serve millions of consumers, small businesses, and corporate, institutional, and government clients.

In April and May 2012, large trading losses occurred at JP Morgan based on transactions done through its London branch. These losses amounted to more than $6 billion.

Yeah, more than $6 billion!

In 2013 they agreed to pay $920 million in fines to US and UK regulators to settle charges related to this London trading debacle which was nicknamed the 'London Whale'.........the errant traders took 'whale-sized' bets that went wrong.

However, in 2015, it seemed like the worst had passed for JP Morgan, and the share price began to rise.

Maybe it was time to jump on board.

In April/May 2015, 1,340 shares were bought in J P Morgan Chase at an all-in cost of €7,760...a sizable purchase.

I felt that this was a real bargain as the bank had a long and successful track record, and I invested more than the usual €5,000 limit.

How did the investment perform?

JP Morgan Chase share price ($)

The share price experienced a strong upward trend in 2016.

To 'bank' these gains, I sold 50% of the holding towards the end of 2016. Then I finished up with a sale of the remaining 50% in 2018 when the share price was north of $107.

Overall, Realized Gains of €2,356 from J P Morgan Chase were achieved, which was a 30%+ return in 3 years.

Misfortunes can lead to fortunes!

Let's go back to Europe...surely a similar recovery was underway.

Let's invest in a French Bank!

Société Générale was France's third largest bank by total assets and sixth largest in Europe.

Dividend Yield

We tend to talk about Dividends using Dividend yield.

This is a % ratio that shows how much a company pays out in Dividends each year, compared to its share price.

The Dividend Yield can be likened to the Interest rate you would receive from the Bank on your deposits.

The target Dividend yield set for my portfolio was a minimum of 3.5% Dividend yield.

It is possible to find well-regarded stocks that have Dividend yields of 4%, 5%, and even 6%.

Yields above 6% could be risky as companies may be paying out more than they can continue to earn.

In July 2015, the **Société Générale** share price was rising…maybe this was the start of something worth buying! The Dividend yield was 4.5% which was attractive.

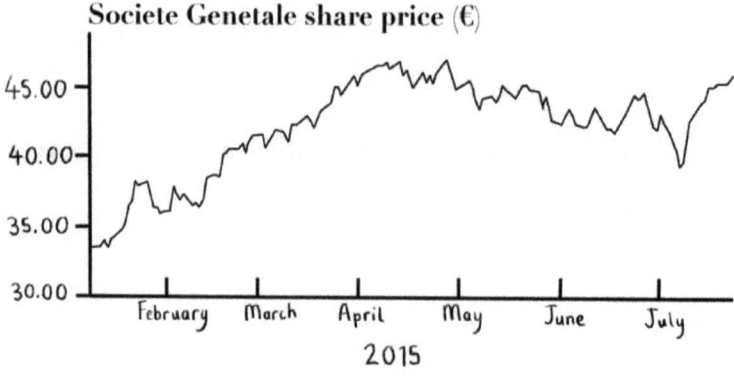

In July 2015, 115 shares were bought at an all-in cost of €5,274. The share price was €45.28 and rising… *let's hop on board!*

How did the share price perform?

It began to fall steeply…...*oops!*

I lost confidence as the price plummeted and **sold out in January 2019 for €28.63 per share realizing losses of -€2,025.**

Not a pretty sight.

I was too scared to stay on board!

What about Spain instead?

The Spanish economy moved into positive territory in 2014 – good news as customers would begin to borrow again and banks would make profits from these loans.

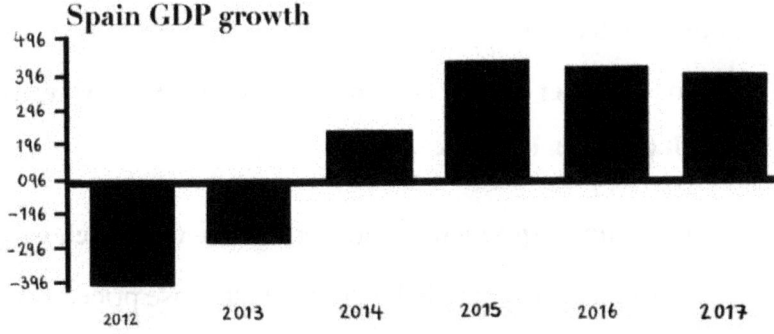

BBVA

BBVA is a multinational Spanish banking group and one of the largest financial institutions in the world.

It operates in Spain, North America, Central and South America and Turkey.

Aha! Buying this share will give me indirect exposure to Central and South America!

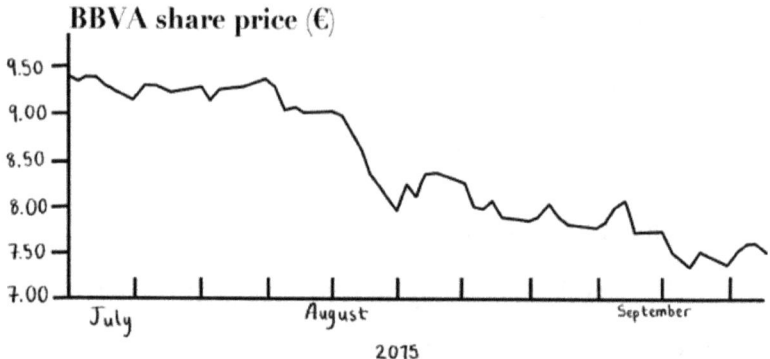

The share price had declined slightly recently, so the timing looked good.

In October 2015, 4,796 shares in BBVA were purchased at a low price.

What has happened to the share since the purchase?

The share price tumbled below the purchase price.

Why did this happen?

The Mexican peso suffered a 14% fall in 2016 upon concerns that newly elected President Trump could rip up a free trade deal with his southern neighbor.

This currency fall contributed to a drop in BBVA profits of nearly 30% in the fourth quarter of 2016.

Hmmm... there's that Central American exposure I was so pleased about!

BBVA's results in Spain were then hit by a one-off regulatory fine of €400 million relating to disputed mortgage clauses.

Too many problems at BBVA. Let's get out!

I sold in February 2018, suffering a loss on sale of -€792.

It could have been worse as the share price continued to fall.

This really underlines the principle of 'always investing in the future, not the past.' If you don't believe the future will be better...better to vamoose!

But where to next?

ING Bank

As the reader may remember, I had made gains from ING Bank earlier, and the share price was now trading at a relatively low point.

ING share price (€)

Should I give it another go?

On 24th May 2016, 460 new shares were purchased at €10.74 each and a cost of €5,031.

Just before the Covid-19 crash, the share price peaked at €12.20, generating **Unrealized Gains of €581 for the portfolio.**

The ING Bank investment also had a Dividend yield of 6.46% on the original cost, which was a strong reason to stay invested.

The largest bank in Italy – Intesa Sanpaolo – now caught my eye.

Intesa Sanpaolo

This Italian bank has 4,500 branches and 12 million customers.

Surely the largest bank in any country would also be the most secure investment.

In May 2017, 1,755 shares were purchased in Intesa Sanpaolo at an all-in cost of €5,063.

How has the share price performed?

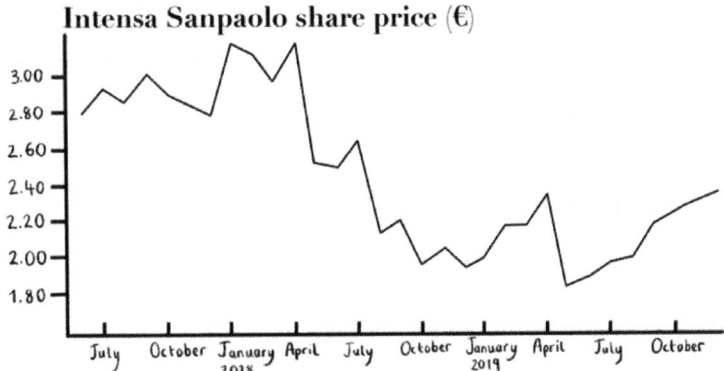

Intensa Sanpaolo share price (€)

By December 2019, the share price had fallen from its purchase price of €2.85 to €2.35, resulting in unrealized capital losses of -€939.

Run or stay?

Since the Global Financial Crisis in 2008, the European Central Bank (ECB) has gradually reduced interest rates across all European banks.

The ECB did this to encourage borrowing/investment. This increased investment would hopefully drive Eurozone economies up to more normal levels.

But a zero-interest rate policy had the effect that banks struggled to make money from their loans.

When the ECB starts to raise interest, banks will become more profitable again, and their share prices are likely to rise.

I decided to view Intesa Sanpaolo as a long-term hold as I took the view that bank share prices would get a material uplift when the ECB started to raise interest rates.

I also decided to have a look at Scandinavian banks with this long-term view.

Nordea Bank:

Nordea is the largest financial services group in the Nordic region and one of the biggest banks in Europe. They had €9.5 billion in operating income and €581.6 billion in assets in 2018.

Nordea offered diversification into Scandinavia for my bank portfolio, and the shares generated an 8% Dividend yield.

Plus, the bank had increased its Dividend in the previous six years…a good track record. The high Dividend yield was risky, but I took a chance.

In February 2018, I bought 560 shares in Nordea for €5,355.

How did the share price perform?

Nordea share price (SEK)

The Nordea share price was stable till October 2018.

Then: it was widely reported that Nordea handled about $790 million in suspicious transactions.

... oops!

This shareholding was sitting on Unrealized Losses, measured in February 2020 against the share price's pre-Covid 19 high of -€791.

Not the kind of Scandinavian drama I want to watch!

I was not ready to sell.... yet!

I was drawn to the high Dividend yield, and I knew interest rates would have to rise eventually, with Nordea in a strong position to benefit from this.

Meanwhile, the Irish economy was performing strongly, and what was good for Ireland was good for Irish banks. Let's have another go at AIB!

AIB

The AIB share price had fallen sharply from €5.62 in early January 2018 to €3.7295 in January 2019.

There did not appear to be any compelling logic for such a significant write down in the share price.

In January 2019, I bought 1,260 shares in AIB for an all-in cost of €4,770.

Like Intesa Sanpaolo and Nordea, this was a purchase for the long haul.

How did the AIB share price perform?

Dismally, with a capital D!

The ECB continued to hold interest rates at very low levels leading to sharply reduced bank revenues at AIB.

Bank lending rates were at all-time lows.

At its pre-Covid price in December 2019, I found I was experiencing Unrealized Losses of -€486.

When you are out of favor, you are out of favor.

I remained convinced that the rationale for staying in Bank shares was still relevant; interest rates would rise... eventually.

Of course, across the pond in North America and Canada, interest rates were higher than those imposed by the European Central Bank.

I looked at one of the 'Big Five' players in the Canadian banking sector: CIBC.

Canadian Imperial Bank of Commerce (CIBC)

CIBC had 11 million clients and 44,000+ employees.

It had total assets of CAD$414.9 billion, and its 2014 net income was CAD$3.2 billion.

On 31st March 2014, I bought 80 shares in Canadian Imperial Bank of Commerce (CIBC) at an all-in cost of €5,080.

How has the share price performed since the purchase?

The share price rose from its purchase price of 95 CAD to a December 2019 high of 112.50 CAD, generating Unrealized Gains of €1,029...also aided by a strengthening of the exchange rate.

The Dividend yield of 6.25% on the original cost was a good reason to stay on board.

UBS (Union Bank of Switzerland)

As of 2017, **UBS** was the 11th largest bank in Europe, with a market capitalization of $64.5 billion.

It had over CHF 3.2 trillion in assets under management.

UBS had a buoyant Fund Management Division, which was not adversely affected by low interest rates.

In the summer of 2019, the UBS share price was moving upwards:

How did the share price perform?

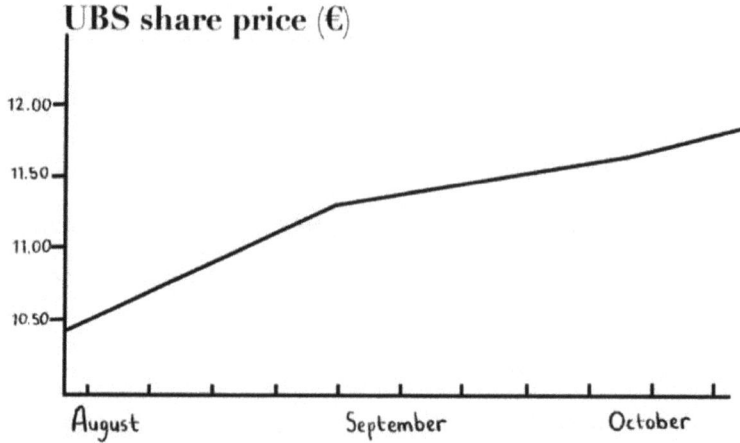

UBS share price (€)

In October 2019, 500 UBS shares were purchased for €5,160.

The share price increased from its purchase price of CHF11.16 to a peak pre-Covid price of CHF13.03, resulting in Unrealized Gains of €955 as of February 2020.

The moneybags in Switzerland know how to manage things!

I decided to have another go at Southern Europe.

Banco Santander

Banco Santander is a leading Spanish bank. It operates in Europe and the Americas and is one of the largest banks in the world by market capitalization. Good Dividends were expected to materialize in time.

In January 2020, 1,300 shares were purchased at a price of €3.86 with an all-in cost of €5,071.

How did the Banco Santander share price perform?

The share rose from its purchase price of €3.86 to €3.953 and pre-Covid, I was sitting on an Unrealized Gain of €68.

Gins and Tonics are cheap in Spain....Slurp! Slurp!

Finally, I decided to take a rest from purchasing Bank shares!

Summary of Realized (cashed in) gains from the sales of Bank shares from 2008 to 2019		
US Banks	Wells Fargo	€3,229
	JP Morgan	€2,356
Irish Banks	Permanent TSB	-€24
	AIB	€1,153
	Bank of Ireland	€2,316
Other	Société Générale	-€2,025
	BBVA	-€792
	ING Bank	€2,051
Total Realized Gains		**€8,264**
Pre-Covid Summary of Unrealized Gains (Based on the market value of shares still held)		
ING Bank	Unrealized Gain	€581
CIBC	Unrealized Gain	€1,029
Intesa Sanpaolo	Unrealized Loss	-939
Nordea Bank	Unrealized Loss	-791
AIB	Unrealized Loss	-486
UBS	Unrealized Gain	€955
Banco Santander	Unrealized Gain	€68
Total Unrealized Gains		**€417**

Overall, net capital gains realized and unrealized, attributable to my portfolio of bank shares, were €8,681.

A job well done, even though I say so myself!

In conclusion

The profit made from bank shares that I bought and sold early on was 'easy peasy' as they were mainly bought as the financial crisis unfolded and share prices were on the floor.

On a number of occasions, I also made currency gains as the shares had been bought when certain currencies were weak.

My experience investing in the banking sector also shows that it was more difficult to make profits from bank investments later in the decade when banks were 'over the worst'.

However, I continued to hold on to the bank shares purchased in the latter half of the 2010-2020 decade.

This is because, as a former banker, I was keenly aware that it had been an unusually challenging trading environment for banks for many years.

Tighter financial regulations imposed since the financial crash and interest rates held at historic lows meant it had been extremely difficult for banks to make satisfactory profits.

But I knew it was likely that Central Banks would soon start to normalize/raise interest rates which would increase bank earnings. This would almost certainly drive bank share prices up more.

We will see what happens.

Banks were an ideal purchase in the aftermath of this market crash. In the next few chapters, our story will reveal other kinds of shares you should buy when you anticipate an improvement in economic conditions.

Chapter Three
Looking to Recovery:
Oil & Basic Resources

Aren't the good times great?

These are the good times when investin' is easy.

Share prices jumpin', and the Dividends are high.

Enjoyin' being rich and spending like crazy'.

Hush out the past, and please don't cry!

(With apologies to Gershwin)

What are the 'good times?

The economic cycle is the usual fluctuating state of a market-based economy.

Economic Cycle

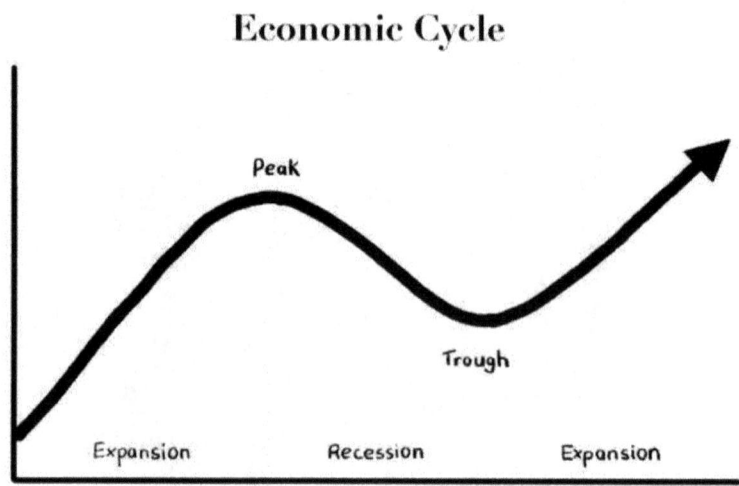

An economy is driven by the activities of Households, Businesses, and Government.

The economy experiences the 'good times' when the economy is expanding towards the peak and the 'bad times' when the economy is falling towards the trough.

To maximize gains from future share price increases, investors need to jump into the stock market as soon as an economy begins to turn from recession towards expansion.

Investors should invest at the very start of the expansion phase and not buy shares when the economy has already expanded, and share prices have already risen.

How can we know when an economy is starting to turn towards growth?

Leading Indicators

'Leading' indicators give signals on future economic trends, and a 'lagging' indicator gives you "the economic trend soon after the trend has been established.

Listen and watch the 'media' for these three leading indicators.

1. ***Economic sentiment.***

What are the economists predicting will happen to the economy? For example, you could look up the EU Economic Sentiment Indicator (ESI) for the sentiment in Europe.

2. ***PMI above 50***

Most countries survey their Purchasing Managers' Intentions (PMI) in terms of the volumes of goods they will buy in the next few months. A PMI above 50 is considered to indicate an economy is heading toward growth.

3. *Consumer sentiment*

There are also indicators of future trends by Households (Consumers). For example, you could look for any changes in the Consumer Sentiment Index to see if consumer spending is likely to increase or decrease, like, are consumers going to buy a car?

So, what shares should we buy when the economy is on the up?

Cyclical stocks involve companies that sell items that consumers buy more of during a booming economy but spend less on during a recession.

Tiffany & Co luxury jewelers would generally be seen as a classic Cyclical stock; they are likely to do more business in the 'good times'and less business in the 'bad times.

In contrast, **Defensive stocks** belong to companies that make or sell items that consumers need to buy regardless of the state of the economy. These shares mostly comprise groceries, medication, and utilities.

As we discovered in Chapter Two, banks are a classic Cyclical stock because banks will make more money if the economy is expanding than if the economy is contracting.

For this reason, when I started to build my portfolio in 2008/9, I invested heavily in *Cyclical* shares, such as bank shares, to gain as the economy started to expand.

Bank shares fall the most when the stock market takes a hit because, in recessionary times, many bank customers are unable to repay their bank loans.

But buying Cyclical shares just after a market crash - when their share prices are at their lowest point - means you stand to profit the most when the economy recovers and share prices go up.

With this in mind, I also began to invest in the highly Cyclical sector of Oil and Basic Resources in 2008 with the belief that buying these shares at their temporarily depressed prices would turn into a very satisfactory profit when the economy and cyclical share prices eventually recovered.

My first foray into oil shares started with a company founded by a fellow Irish man.

God bless us…an "Oirish" share!

Why invest in Tullow Oil?

Tullow Oil was a leading independent oil and gas exploration and production company with 90 exploration and production licenses across 16 countries.

They maintained 34 Oil producing fields and employed 1,152 people.

The share price had declined in mid-2008 but was starting to show signs of turning back up. This could be a good time to buy.

692 Tullow Oil Shares were bought in 2008 for £7 each at an all-in cost of £5,057.

How did the share price perform since the purchase?

Marvelously...!

However, in January 2011, the Dividend yield had fallen to 0.5%.

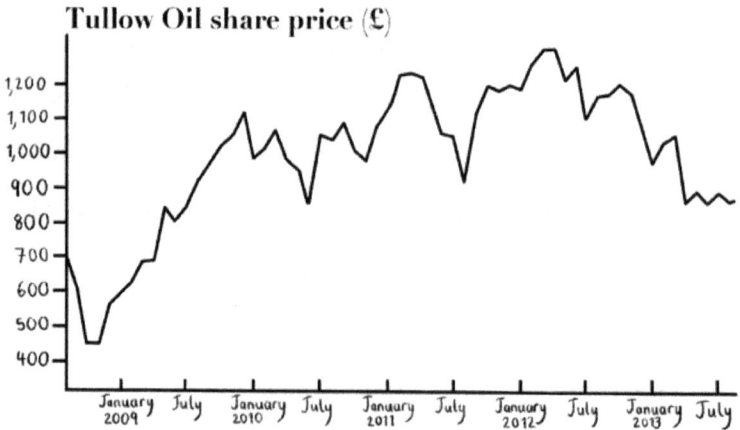

Dividend yields typically fall when the company doesn't increase the Dividend pay-out as fast as the share price is rising.

What this means is that the Dividend becomes a smaller and smaller percentage of the increasing share price.

At 0.5%, the Dividend for Tullow Oil was far below my Dividend target of 3.5%+, so I decided to sell 400 Tullow Oil shares at £12+ a share.

Not only was this cashing in some of the profits by selling at a higher share price, but I could now reinvest these newly generated profits in other shares that were offering a higher Dividend yield and thus generate more income for myself.

After this sale, I noticed that the share price momentum for Tullow Oil was continuing downward, and so I decided, in 2013, when the Dividend yield was still inadequate at just 1.5%, to sell the remaining 292 shares at £8.50+ per share.

Should I have sold earlier when the share was £12+?

Things often look different when viewed through a rear-view mirror!

Overall, the portfolio profited to the tune of €3,777 from Tullow Oil.

And, as it turned out, the decision to exit Tullow Oil in 2011 and 2013 was 'heaven sent.'

If the Tullow Oil shares had not been sold till later, when the share price had fallen to £2, I would have lost my shirt and my knickers as well!

Tullow Oil share price (£)

52

What caused the collapse in the share price?

As expected, because of the economic recovery post 2008/9, there was a huge demand for oil.

The oil price reached $110 per barrel in 2012, but this insatiable demand encouraged large increases in oil production, and so the market was flooded with oil from 2014 onwards.

The Oil price fell dramatically and averaged c.$50 in 2016, causing Tullow Oil to fall as low as £2 a share from 2016 onwards.

Of course, back then, I did not foresee this collapse in the oil price coming! Back in 2013, I wanted even more exposure to oil shares to profit from the then-recovering global economy, so off I went looking for more oil shares.

Total Oil

Total Oil is a major French oil company. The business covers the entire oil and gas chain, from crude oil and natural gas exploration and production to power generation, transportation, refining, petroleum product marketing, and international crude oil and product trading.

Total Oil is also a chemicals manufacturer and a player in low-carbon energies.

In 2013, the share price was €44.50, and the Dividend yield was 4%+.

In December 2013, I bought 100 Total Oil shares for €4,506.

What happened to the Total Oil share price since the purchase?

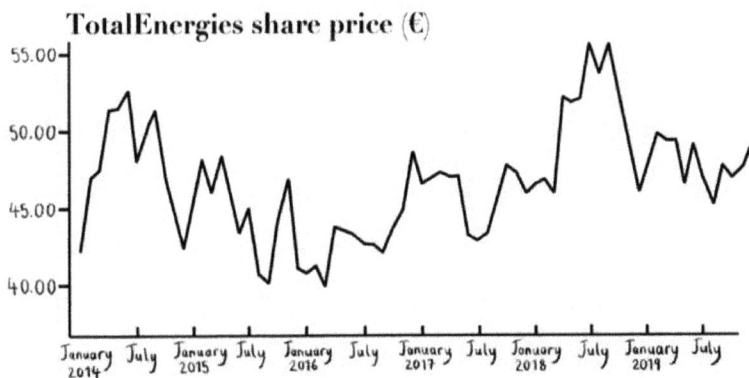

TotalEnergies share price (€)

A lot of ups and downs!

Thankfully Total did not suffer the same momentous decline as Tullow Oil experienced in 2014 due to the more diverse energy activities undertaken by the French company.

In fact, Total Oil recently changed its name to **TotalEnergies**, to emphasize that it is transforming the company from total reliance on the production of Fossil fuels into other forms of energy, such as Renewables.

In December 2019, the share price at its pre-Covid peak had moved up by 10%, and the Dividend yield was above 5%.

I was sitting on an Unrealized Capital Gain of €414.

However, it was an unpredictable performer.

I was learning a very valuable lesson for those interested in oil shares.

Much of the oil is produced by a small number of countries (OPEC+) who act together and sometimes flood the market with oil.

These same countries also act together to reduce production and cause a scarcity of oil which results in a large increase in the oil price.

Geopolitical risks, such as wars, coups d'état, and government changes, can also affect the oil price and the value of oil shares.

Therefore, stock market investors often see major increases and collapse in oil prices that are unrelated to market demand.

All this makes Oil a very volatile share to hold which does <u>not</u> always behave like a Cyclical share.

I lost interest in Oil!

In 2015, I decided to expand my portfolio to include Basic Resources.

The Basic Resources sector is composed of companies involved in the discovery, extraction, and processing of raw materials such as mining, forestry, and chemicals.

These companies often produce 'commodities,' which are physical goods trading at a standardized price subject to market demand, Examples of commodities you might know include gold, grains, gas, lumber, coffee, cotton, and sugar.

Every industry needs raw materials (or commodities) if they want to make and sell products to their customers. So, if the economy is on the up and consumers start to buy in the shops again, the demand for raw materials to make shop goods goes up.

The value of non-oil commodities goes up or down based on market supply and demand for the good rather than the actions of a special interest group like OPEC+. In this way, Basic Resources Companies can be viewed as genuine Cyclical shares.

In 2015, the global economic recovery was looking increasingly solid, and so I went looking for a suitable company to invest in.

I decided to go for a stock mining a commodity such as copper that had industrial uses rather than a company focused on resources that were used solely in consumer products.

Surely there will always be a demand for copper.

Antofagasta

Antofagasta is a Chilean copper mining group that was incorporated in London in 1888. They have longevity and know how to handle the ups and downs of the copper market.

I was interested in broadening my exposure, not only to commodities such as copper but geographically to South America.

I took a relatively small stake in Antofagasta to gain experience in owning shares in a company that produced commodities.

Was it a good time to buy?

Copper prices had been declining steadily for a number of years, and by 2015, the copper price had not been at such a low level since early 2009.

In 2015, growth forecasts from the World Bank for the health of the global economy were not as optimistic as they had previously been.

Demand for copper, which is used across industries from construction to car manufacturing, had suffered from the slowing Chinese economy.

I saw that the Antofagasta share price was declining in 2015.

The Dividend yield was low, and the intention was to hold short term, as I viewed the stock as genuinely Cyclical, which I would sell when the economy recovered.

In August 2015, I bought 350 shares in Antofagasta at £5.79 each at a cost of €2,861.

I wouldn't usually purchase such a small holding, but because I had no experience with copper or South America particularly, I decided to go small with the purchase.

How did it go?

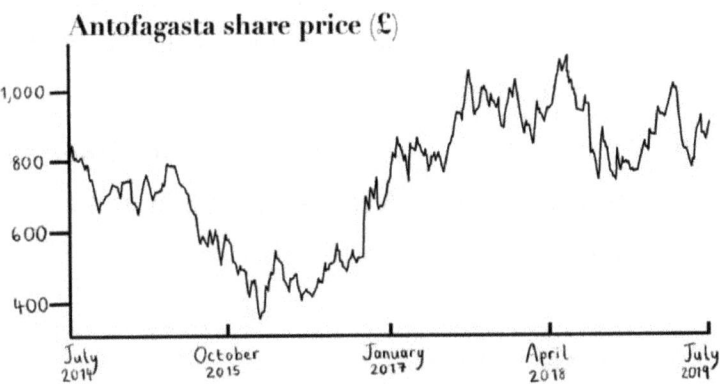

The share price rose steadily in line with economic growth!

In March 2018, I sold Antofagasta at a price of £8.80 and realized a capital gain of €578 (+20%)

Very pleasant indeed!

58

Buoyed by the experience in copper, I decided to go for a company with plenty of different commodity products to sell.

Rio Tinto

Rio Tinto is one of the world's largest metals and mining corporations.

While primarily focused on the extraction of Base Metals, Rio Tinto also has significant refining operations, mainly bauxite and iron ore. The company is mostly concentrated in Australia and Canada.

In 2018, Rio Tinto had a generous Dividend Yield of 5%+.

I was attracted to the company's very significant presence in Australia and Canada as these countries are less risky than South America.

In March 2018, I used the proceeds from the Antofagasta sale to buy 80 Rio Tinto shares at an all-in cost of €3,390.

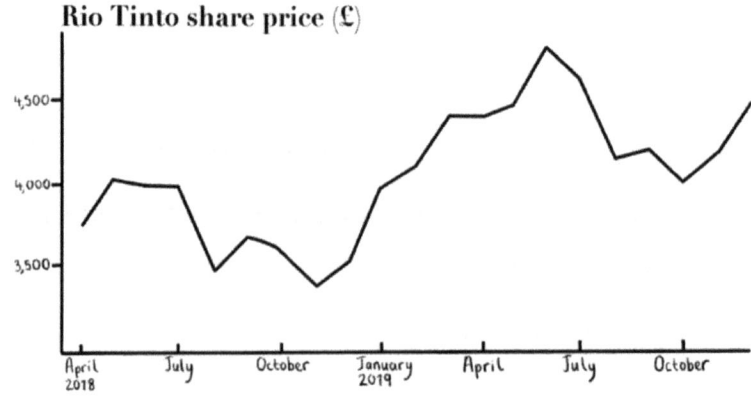

Rio Tinto share price (£)

How did the Rio Tinto share price perform?

Looking at its pre-Covid peak, I was experiencing an Unrealized Gain of €2,178.

Plus, Rio Tinto's Dividend yield was by then a very attractive 5.8%.

Encouraged, I went prospecting for more mining companies… geddit?

BHP Group

BHP, formerly known as BHP Billiton, is an Anglo-Australian multinational mining, metals, and petroleum company.

In 2019, the Dividend Yield was an attractive 5.2%

In November 2019, I bought 330 BHP shares, at £16.882 each, for €6,595.

What happened to the BHP share price afterward?

The share rose satisfactorily to a pre-Covid high of £18.52.

At that point, the Unrealized Gain from the BHP holding was €577.

Positive anyway! More commodities, please!

Hey, what do you know about Chemical companies? 'Uh…nuthin'!

BASF

BASF SE is a European chemical company and the largest chemical producer in the world.

In 2015, the company employed more than 122,000 people.

BASF posted sales of €70.4 billion and net income of €6.7 billion for 2015.

Despite this success, I noticed that the share price was on a downward trend as it decreased from a year high of €92.55 in March 2015 to the purchase price of €73.63 in early December 2015.

The Dividend Yield at the time of purchase was 4.1%.

In December 2015, I purchased 71 shares in BASF, costing €5,284.

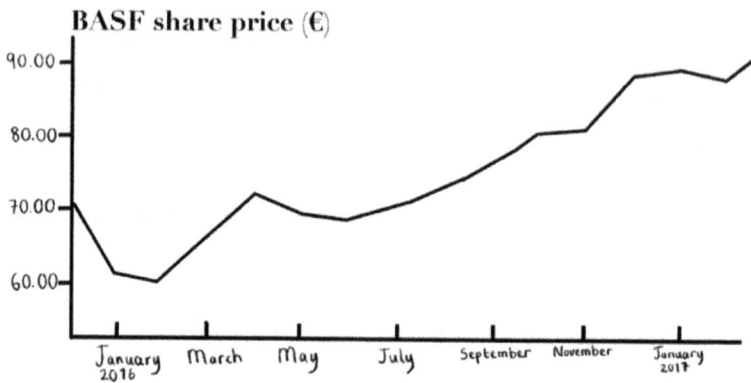

By January 2017, good news....the share price had risen to €89+.

However, the Dividend yield had declined to 3.1% by 2017, which was relatively unattractive.

So, I decided to sell some to achieve a higher Dividend yield elsewhere.

I sold a small lot in February 2017, 15 of my 71 shares, at a price of €89.03, yielding a profit of €178.

How did the BASF share price perform since February 2017?

Badly!

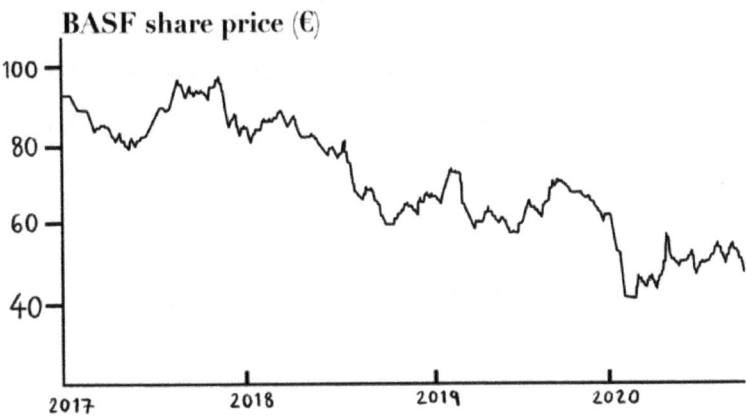

At its pre-Covid peak, in January 2020, I was nursing Unrealized Losses of -€396 on my remaining holding.

Why continue to hold the shares?

Based on the original purchase price, the Dividend yield - which had been increased over the years despite the fall in the share price - remained at an attractive 5%.

Where next?

Covestro – a German Company

Covestro produces polyurethane and polycarbonate raw materials, which are suitable long lasting and environmentally friendly replacements for conventional materials such as steel and glass.

In early 2020, the share was at a relatively low point, and the Dividend yield of 6.43% was a major attraction.

In February 2020, I bought 86 Covestro shares at a price of €38.95, totaling all in €3,393.

One week later, the Covestro share price reached its pre-Covid high, and I was sitting on a small Unrealized Gain of €148.

The overall performance of the Oil & Basic Resources sectors up to the arrival of Covid:

Summary	Oil & Basic Resources		(€)
Tullow Oil	Realized Gain	London	3,777
Antofagasta	Realized Gain	London	578
	Total Realized Gains	London	4,355
Rio Tinto	Unrealized Gain	London	2,178
BHP Group	Unrealized Gain	London	577
	Total Unrealized Gains	London	2,755
	Total Gains	London	7,110
BASF	Unrealized Loss	Frankfurt	-396
Covestro	Unrealized Gain	Frankfurt	148
Total Oil	Unrealized Gain	Paris	414
	Total Unrealized Gains	Frankfurt/ Paris	166
BASF	Realized Gain	Frankfurt	178
	Total Gains	Frankfurt/ Paris	344
	Total Gains	Oil & Basic Resources	7,454

In conclusion

From my investments in Oil & Basic Resources companies, I achieved net gains of €7,454 and an ongoing Dividend yield of 7%.

Buying Cyclicals (especially oil) at a low point in the economic cycle proved to be a shrewd investment.

This is because Cyclical shares tend to perform more strongly than the other shares in the market when economies are in recovery mode.

Some investors use this as a key investing strategy - switching in and out of Cyclicals depending on whether the economy is in a growth or decline phase.

But as we saw, for Tullow Oil, it was a different story. The Tullow Oil share price declined significantly as the oil price collapsed due to massive oversupply.

I learned a very valuable lesson from my experience in Tullow Oil: You never lose when you sell at a profit!

If you are interested in investing in Oil, remember that it is not only a highly Cyclical share but also that oil prices are affected by the actions of OPEC+ cutting or boosting supply.

Political problems in producer countries such as Libya, Iran, and Venezuela can also sometimes worsen these issues.

In that sense, the relationship between the oil share price and the economic cycle is not as straightforward as it is with other Basic Resources.

With Basic Resources such as copper, we saw that, as the economy recovered, demand for these commodities increased, making this a profitable sector overall.

It's not foolproof, though, as some of these kinds of companies can be affected by geopolitical risk, just like Oil.

And agricultural commodities, such as grains and cotton, have additional worries, such as weather, disease, and pests. So always keep an eye on these stocks in your portfolio!

This was a job in which I was well pleased!

In the next chapter, I will outline another shrewd strategy that pays off handsomely when investing in Cyclical stocks: Buy a share that is unloved by everybody but yourself...!

Chapter Four
Investing for the 'Good Times':
The Automobile Industry

"Walkies?"

Toyota

In 2010 I was interested in investing in the Automobile industry, which is considered a Cyclical share with more cars being bought in the good times when consumers have more money to spend.

I wanted to invest in a reliable company and ideally achieve some geographical diversification in my holdings.

I knew that the Japanese Car manufacturer, Toyota, has a world-famous manufacturing system. The system works intelligently and eliminates waste so that only minimal inventory is needed.

The system is also known by the more generic terms 'lean manufacturing' and 'just-in-time production'.

Toyota had interesting new products coming on stream and was maintaining a seeming lead in new hybrid engine technologies, such as those used in the high-profile Prius.

However, the share was in trouble!

In January 2010, Toyota announced recalls of approximately 5.2 million vehicles for a pedal entrapment/floor mat problem and an additional 2.3 million vehicles for an accelerator pedal problem. Eventually, the total number of cars that the company was forced to recall amounted to 9 million vehicles! The number of alleged victims and reported problems also sharply increased following the recall announcements.

Unsurprisingly, in August 2011, the share price was at a relatively low point:

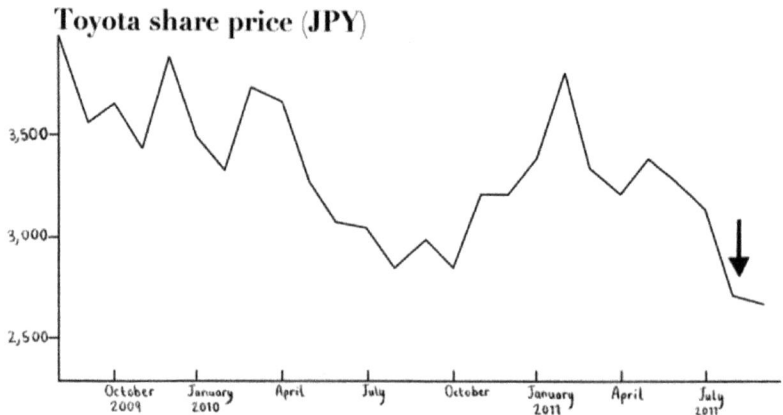

Toyota share price (JPY)

I reckoned that a long-standing reputable manufacturer such as Toyota would *'weather the Recall storm'* and bounce back to business as usual in time.

So, the low share price of JPY2,639 represented a buying opportunity.

In August 2011, I purchased 121 Toyota shares for €3,307.

The Dividend yield was very low, so the intention was to hold the share for the short term only and ideally sell profitably as the price returned to normal.

How did the share price perform after the purchase?

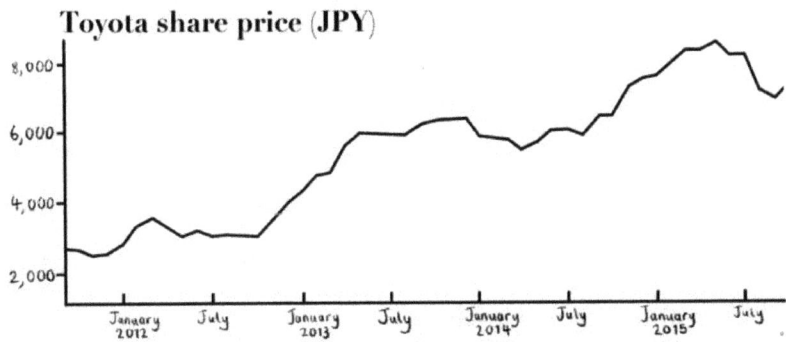

Very well!

By 2015, the share price had risen dramatically.

The sale of Toyota shares

At this time, the Dividend yield was a paltry 2.17%, so I decided to sell a small number of shares to get higher Dividends elsewhere.

On the 16th of September 2015, I sold 25 Toyota shares generating a capital profit of €611.

I was reluctant to sell the remainder of the holding as the stock provided some geographic diversification.

Toyota was the only investment held at that time, in the portfolio, in the 'Land of the Rising Sun'.

The Toyota share price, at its pre-Covid peak, continued to be ahead of cost, generating very significant **Unrealized Gains of €3,510**

The overall gain, including the €611 realized from the earlier sale, amounted to €4,121... *a big win!*

We are the champions...of the Stock Exchange (Queen misquoted)

I was eager to buy more shares in Automobile Companies.

In early 2015, I noticed that the US dollar had strengthened considerably.

US $ / Euro Exchange Rate

In 2014 $1 was worth €0.75, but it had increased to €0.85 by 2015.

A strong dollar should encourage Americans to buy more high-end German cars like BMWs ('Beamers') as they were getting 10 cents more for each dollar when they converted to Euros.

And for an investor, the BMW Dividend yield was an OK 3.5%.

BMW

Could I make money from a BMW investment?

The BMW share price was relatively stable in 2014, even though profits grew by 10.3% during that year.

All the signs were good!

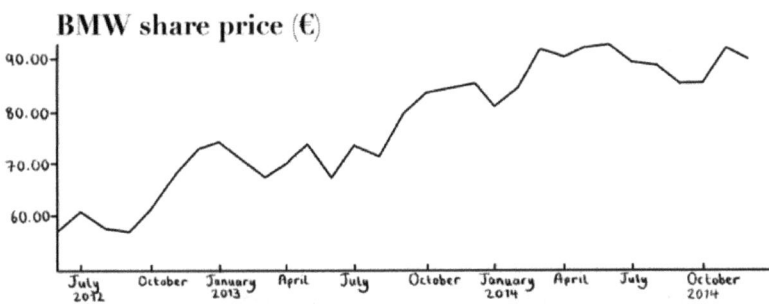

In January 2015, 56 shares were purchased in BMW at a price of €87.95, for €4,980.

How did the BMW share price perform since the purchase?

Very well until a newly elected President Trump picked on German cars as a target in his protectionist 'Buy US' politics.

BMW's share price fell, and it remained in the doldrums…

Time to hit the road…

I sold at the beginning of October 2019 and Realized Losses of -€1,352

The share price rose steeply between October and December 2019. …if only I had held on to the shares till then.

BMW share price (after the sale) €

However, if I had held on later, till Spring 2020, the share price would have been even lower than the sale price achieved in October.

Never be afraid to cut your losses and sell.

Daimler

Daimler is one of the biggest producers of premium cars (such as Mercedes) and the world's biggest manufacturer of commercial vehicles with a global reach.

Daimler's share price was at a low of €63 in April 2016.

Daimler's Dividend yield was an attractive 5.58%.

In April 2016, 80 shares in Daimler were purchased for €5,065.

How did the Daimler share price perform since the purchase?

As with BMW, President Trump wanted to make America great again at Daimler's expense! The share price declined...

It was time to exit the stock, and the Daimler holding was sold on 13th February 2020 at a price of €43.03, realizing losses of -€1,667.

Volkswagen

Volkswagen is a German motor vehicle manufacturer. It was the largest car maker by worldwide sales in 2016 and 2017.

Despite the previous two German auto investments going wrong, I decided to look at VW, given its recent strong earnings performance.

Surely VW would not break down on me!

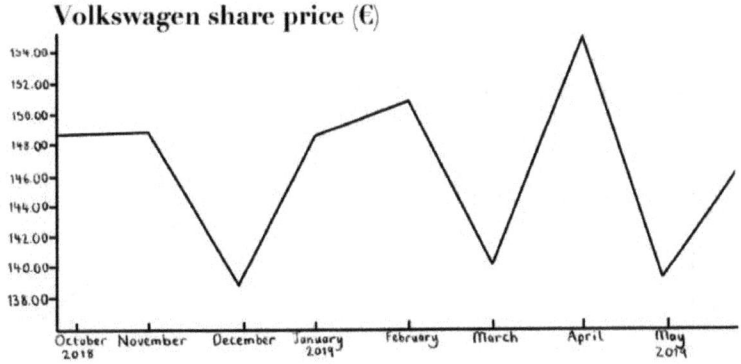

In May 2019, the share price was at a relatively low point of €146.

The Dividend yield was just OK, at 3.5%, but I was hoping to make profits as the share price improved.

On 21ˢᵗ May 2019, 34 VW shares were purchased for €5,032.

The share price rose dramatically in a matter of months to reach its pre-Covid peak of €176.24 compared with €146.45 at purchase.

I was sitting on Unrealized Gains of €960.

Success from at least one German Auto

What about Auto components rather than the cars themselves?

Bridgestone Corp

Bridgestone is the world's largest tire and rubber company.

On 23rd May 2019, 150 Bridgestone shares were bought for €5,078.

The Dividend Yield was almost 4% at the time.

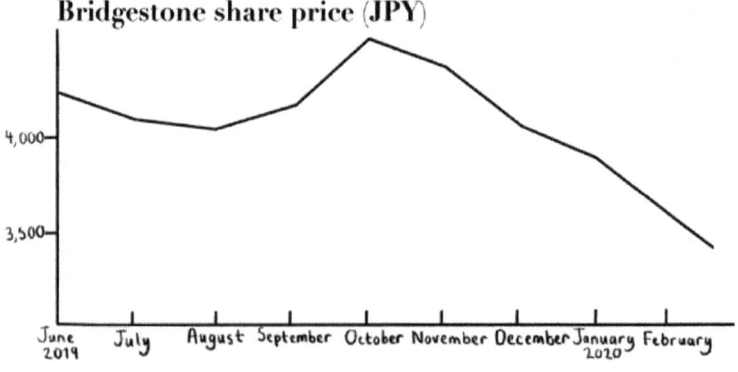

Bridgestone share price (JPY)

Most other shares were experiencing pre-Covid rises but, for some reason, not Bridgestone!

Thankfully, due to a stronger Japanese Yen, I was only facing modest Unrealized Losses of -€178.

The share price rose satisfactorily......

....to...... You lucky boy!........

Pre-Covid Feb-20 Summary of Autos shareholdings performance		
BMW	Realized Losses	-1,352
Daimler	Realized Losses	-1,667
Volkswagen	Unrealized Gain	960
German cars net losses		-2,059
Bridgestone Corp	Unrealized Losses	-178
Toyota	Unrealized Gain	3,510
Toyota	Realized Gain	611
Japan net gains		3,943
Auto Sector	Net Gains	1,884

Lessons learned.

Automobiles can be seen as a genuinely Cyclical share in that the share price will go up when the economy is growing.

But my experience in this sector was that significant damage could be caused by the words and actions of politicians like Donald Trump... *so-called political risk!*

I also witnessed how favorable movements in currency sometimes help mitigate losses.

And interestingly, how one shareholding can save the day! (Thank you, Toyota)

Up to now, I have shared my experience in the purchases of Cyclical Stocks, which usually do well when the economy is recovering.

That's because the Global Financial Crisis of 2007-08 presented an opportunity to invest in these Cyclical shares, which had been beaten down.

But a well-diversified portfolio must also contain Defensive Shares that tend to do better than the market when the market is starting to fall.

The next few Chapters will deal with my experience investing in Defensive Stocks across various industries.

They are the 'safe bets' for the 'bad times.

Chapter Five
Investing for the 'Bad Times':
Pharmaceuticals

"Time to invest in pharmaceuticals"

Knowing whether economies are in a recession or enjoying growth is vital information for any investor when considering buying or selling shares.

That's because there are shares that will hold most of their value during recessions: These are called 'Defensive' shares.

Thems the ones to buy when the bad times are comin'

Defensive stocks are companies that make or sell the products that we must use even when money is tight.

For example, prescription drugs, groceries, and utility bills must be paid for regardless of the overall state of the economy.

Granny needs her medications in good times and bad!

From 2008 onwards, having witnessed the stock markets crater, I took the opportunity to buy many Cyclical shares such as Banks, Oil, Basic Resources, and Automobiles.

But readers will remember the great uncertainty that existed at the time around the full extent of the subprime mortgage crisis contagion.

With the future so hard to predict, at this time, I also decided to take refuge in the safety of a very stable Defensive sector:

Pharmaceuticals (Pharma).

Due to the uncertain headwinds in the global economy, I deliberately looked for shares in large reputable pharmaceutical companies that had a long history of bringing highly successful drugs to market.

Pfizer

Pfizer Inc. is a US pharmaceutical company that is engaged in the discovery, development, and manufacture of healthcare products. Its portfolio includes vaccines and consumer healthcare products.

Pfizer's well-known brands include Lipitor and Viagra.

Lipitor cleans the veins, and Viagra fills them!

Pfizer maintained a barely acceptable Dividend yield of 3.5%+

I was attracted to the pedigree and safety of the share.

In August 2008, 200 Pfizer shares, at $21.85 each, were bought for €3,646.

Then, in 2013, Pfizer floated its animal health division, called Zoetis, as a public company on the German stock market.

24 shares of my Pfizer holding were converted into Zoetis shares, and, as this holding was very small, I decided to sell it.

The Zoetis shares were sold on 28th April 2015 at a profit of €523.

(The Zoetis shares were sold at double the value of the original Pfizer shares). *Well done to the Board of Pfizer.*

I am sure you will agree!

Meanwhile, the Pfizer share price remained on a gentle upward trend, but the 3.33% Dividend was unappealing to someone for whom the annual income from Dividends is an important supplement to their income.

I sold 44 shares in Pfizer in October 2018 at a share price of $42.34, which Realized Gains amounting to €815.

I used this profit to switch to shares that paid higher Dividends.

My remaining Pfizer shares had Unrealized Gains of €2,456 in February 2020 (pre-Covid peak).

Adding the Realized and Unrealized Gains together, the overall gain from Pfizer was €3,794, which demonstrated the safety of investing in well-established, highly respected Defensive stocks during times of economic uncertainty.

Sure, what do you expect from a pharma that starts with a silent pee?

I went looking for other US Pharma companies.

AbbVie

AbbVie are focused on chronic autoimmune diseases in rheumatology, gastroenterology, and oncology, including blood cancers, virology, hepatitis C virus, HIV, Parkinson's disease, multiple sclerosis, thyroid disease, and cystic fibrosis.

AbbVie employs 28,000 people and sells medicines in 170+ countries.

The AbbVie share price had been enjoying a good run in early 2016, and I was attracted to it.

AbbVie's Revenues of $25.560 Bn had grown by 13.3% in that year.

In April 2016, 40 AbbVie shares were purchased at a cost of €2,197.

The Dividend yield was low, but their new drugs were very promising.

How did the AbbVie share price perform since the purchase?

The share price, pre-Covid, in December 2019 was $88, much higher than the purchase price of $61, representing Unrealized profits of €999.

A great grand!

I could have sold my holding to cash in this profit, but the 5.02% Dividend Yield now being paid out by AbbVie was an incentive to stay in.

However, for further investments in this sector, I was keen to diversify away from US Pharma.

Switzerland has a high reputation for Pharma, and the Swiss Franc is considered a very safe currency.

Roche Pharmaceuticals

Roche AG is a Swiss multinational healthcare company that operates worldwide. It is the third-largest Pharma company in the world.

The company develops medicines for oncology, immunology, infectious diseases, ophthalmology, and neuroscience.

Roche's revenues in fiscal year 2016 were 50.58 billion Swiss Francs (CHF).

Roche has also increased their Dividend every year for 30 years.

In 2017 there was an upward trend in the share price

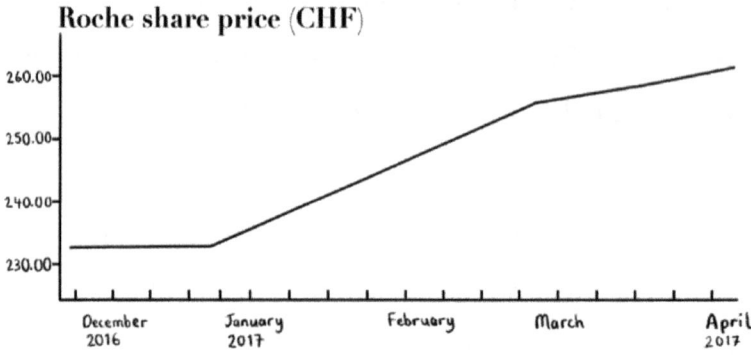

So, in April, I purchased 20 shares at CHF 260 per share with an all-in cost of €4,889.

What happened to the Roche share price since the purchase?

Roche share price after the sale (CHF)

A year later, in April 2018, the share price had declined by 15%.

In January 2019, it climbed back to the purchase price of CHF 260 but then started to decline yet again.

I lost faith in the company, and two years after buying the share, I exited the shareholding in April 2019, resulting in a Realized Loss on the transaction of -€110.

This small loss arose due to transaction charges incurred on the sale.

Was the sale of Roche in April 2019 a good idea?

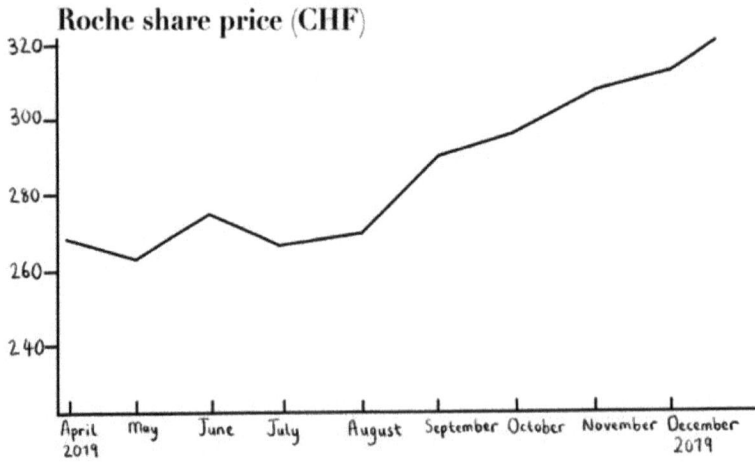

When I sold, the share price was CHF 270, but almost immediately afterward, it climbed upward, reaching a pre-Covid peak of CHF 320 by February 2020.

Not my finest hour...!

Thankfully the other pharmaceutical shares performed strongly and, looking at the Pharma sector overall, pre-Covid, the Realized and Unrealized Gains amounted to €4,683:

Pfizer	Realized Gain	€1,338
Pfizer	Unrealized Gain	€2,456
AbbVie	Unrealized Gain	€999
Roche	Realized Gain	-€110

In addition, the Dividend yield on the unsold shares, calculated using the original cost, was a hugely satisfactory 8.67%.

Outlook

The overall trend for pharmaceutical companies is positive, given people are living longer than before, requiring more and more sophisticated pharmaceutical products to maintain their health.

Plus, these companies generally pay attractive Dividends to their shareholders.

As a buy-and-hold Defensive investment, Pharma stocks make a compelling case.

The only downside to this sector is when an economy starts to take off in a 'boom' time. Pharma stocks will not increase dramatically in price like Cyclical shares. The upside from your Pharma holdings as we head towards the good times will be more gradual.

Any more Defensive shares…how about Utilities?

Chapter Six

Protecting Against the Downside:

Utility Companies

"Ah please can we turn on the heating"

Utility companies are considered Defensive because their numbers of customers don't change too much depending on the economic weather: People need to use energy in good times and bad.

In addition, the prices that Utility companies can charge customers are fixed by national regulators. This fixed income allows the utility company to make investments in large-scale utility infrastructures like electricity and gas connectivity and interconnectors, oil and gas pipelines, and renewables.

The fixed price also means that profits are effectively guaranteed. Therefore, the Dividends offered by Utility companies are a safe bet for investors.

So where to start with a utility company?

National Grid

National Grid is one of the world's largest investor-owned utilities, and it owns and operates the electricity transmission network in England and Wales. It also owns and operates the gas National Transmission System in Great Britain. In the US, it distributes energy in Massachusetts, New York, and Rhode Island.

The Dividend yield, at the time of purchase in 2010, was 5%+.

In 2010, the share price was falling!

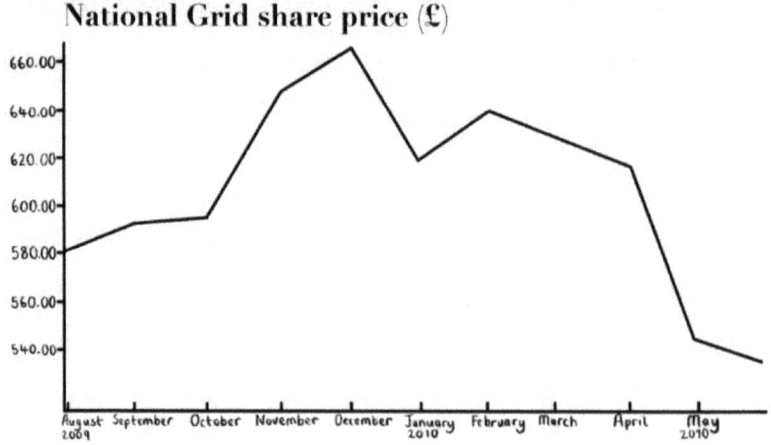

National Grid share price (£)

I purchased 889 National Grid shares in July 2010 at £5.09 each, resulting in an all-in cost of €5,900.

How did the share price perform (after the purchase)?

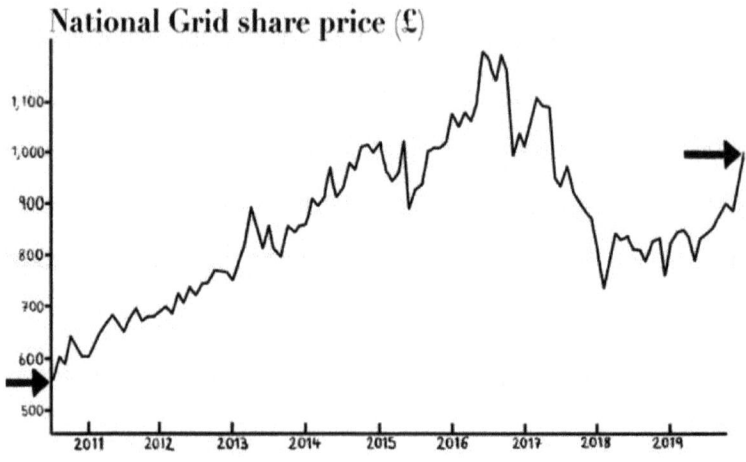

National Grid share price (£)

The purchase was very well-timed!

The share price increased in value very satisfactorily and, at its pre-Covid peak in February 2020, showed an Unrealized Gain of €5,448.

All in all, the investment was a great success story.

I considered these shares a long-term hold as both Dividends and its share price continued to grow.

I was becoming attracted to other UK Utilities.

SSE PLC

SSE supplies energy, phone, and broadband to UK homes as well as boiler cover.

SSE invests £1.5bn a year and employs 20,000 people to develop and maintain its energy infrastructure.

The SSE Dividend Yield was 6%...*good for my annual vacations!*

The trend in the share price was strongly upward in 2014.

In June 2014, 250 SSE shares were purchased at £15.679, resulting in an all-in cost of €4,941.

The SSE share price declined steadily since its purchase in 2014!

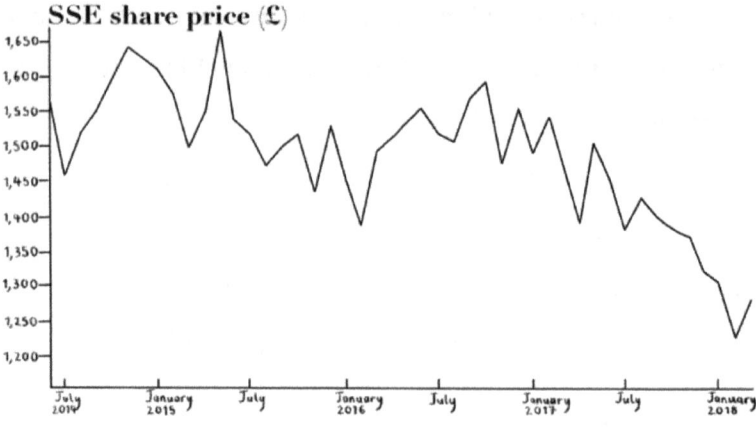

The trend was not my friend!

Sale of SSE

In March 2018, the SSE shares were sold at a price of £12 per share, which Realized Losses on the day of -€1,489.

Centrica

Centrica supplies energy and services to over 25 million customers, mainly in the UK, Ireland, and North America, through strong brands, all supported by around 15,000 engineers and technicians.

The share price level looked cheap in March/April 2016:

91

The Dividend Yield was 5%+ which encouraged a purchase.

In May 2016, I purchased 2,500 Centrica shares at a cost of €6,421.

Dividends of 5%+ from a regulated industry like Utilities? What could go wrong?

Did Centrica fare any better than SSE?

Nope!

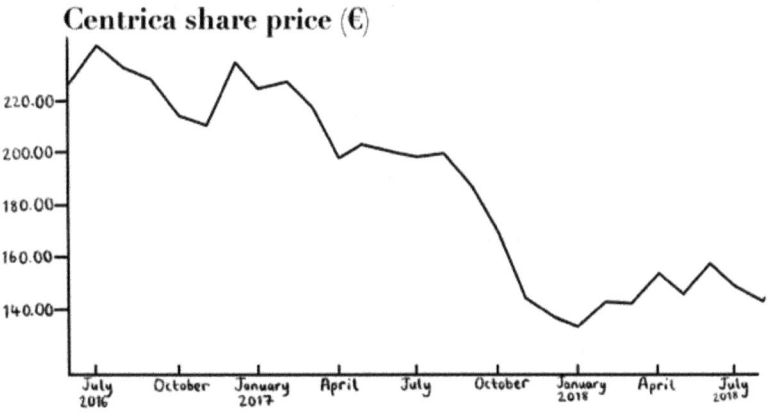

Sale of Centrica

The Centrica share price fell by 30% due to rumors that they would have to cut their Dividend.

What caused such a massive decline in these UK Utilities' share prices?

'It's just not right that two-thirds of energy customers are stuck on the most expensive tariffs."

UK Prime Minister Theresa May, October 2016.

A probe by the Competition and Markets Authority discovered that UK customers overpay on their energy bills by £1.4 billion a year.

So, the Regulators then set different maximum prices for energy in each region.

The new law included limits on Standard Variable Tariffs, the default rates consumers revert to once fixed-term contracts expire, which still covered two-thirds of the market.

This was followed by a price cap for prepay meter users.

Then bills were capped for households on a standard dual fuel tariff which saved the average family £100 a year.

Company earnings for UK Utilities evaporated…as did the value of their share prices.

No future in sticking with this troubled sector…. Let's cut our losses.

I decided to sell my holdings in Centrica in August 2018 as there seemed to be plenty of downside on the way and no upside.

The £1.44 sale price generated a *nasty* loss of -€2,435.

Ochone, ochone!

The sale was painful, but despite the Realized Loss, the share price continued downward since the sale, falling almost by another 40% to £0.88p (at their pre-Covid 'peak').

Thank God I wasn't afraid to cut my losses and sell.

Lessons Learnt

The UK Regulatory Authorities, egged on by UK politicians, had made sure that SSE and Centrica prices were held in check. This move would have pleased ordinary energy customers (voters) in the UK.

National Grid UK has so far escaped the wrath of politicians because their customers are not voters but other UK Utility Companies (such as SSE and Centrica).

With UK energy prices continuing to be 'politically charged', I decided to look overseas.

The next investment was in Canada, far away from the UK.

Enbridge Inc

Enbridge Inc is a Canadian multinational pipeline company focusing on the transportation of crude oil and natural gas.

I have included it as a Utility as they must build and protect their pipelines in the same way as Utilities build and protect their infrastructure.

An important feature of pipeline companies is that they work with long-term contracts, which gives them a very stable income, like Utilities.

Enbridge's expansive pipeline system is the longest in North America, with over 5,000 kilometers of pipelines in Canada and the United States.

Enbridge moves 25% of the crude oil produced in North America and transports 20% of the natural gas consumed in the U.S.

The company had also been an early investor in renewable energy.

In January 2019, I purchased 110 shares in Enbridge Inc, resulting in an all-in cost of €3,351. The Dividend Yield was 6%.

How has the share price performed since the purchase?

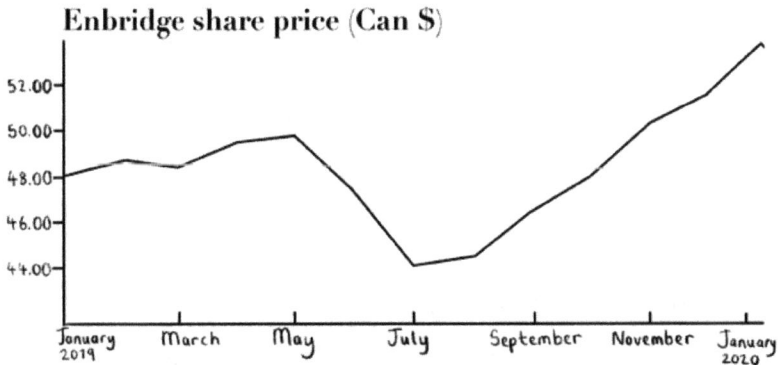

Enbridge share price (Can $)

The share price rose from CAD $45.34 to a pre-Covid peak of CAD $53.81, up almost 20% within a year, generating **an Unrealized Gain of €606**…a very good result indeed.

Isn't it great that the Canadian Mounties are in control?

Greencoat Renewables

Greencoat Renewables PLC is an Irish company investing primarily in Irish and European wind farms and renewable energy infrastructure.

In September 2019, 4,320 shares in Greencoat Renewables were purchased at €1.15 per share, resulting in an all-in cost of €5,006.

The Dividend yield was 5%.

How did the share perform since the purchase?

The share price rose to €1.21 in a few months, resulting n an **Unrealized Gain of €221**. Not bad.

Where to next? Any opportunities on the Iberian Peninsula?

Energias de Portugal SA (EDP)

EDP owns significant electricity generating and distribution assets.

Their business includes complementary areas, such as water, gas, laboratory testing, vocational training, and real estate management.

It also has a major presence in the United States, Brazil, Africa, and Macau............. where *in god's name is Macau?*

In November 2019, EDP announced that it had reached a 50/50 Joint Venture agreement with the French gas and power company Engie SA to merge their fixed and floating offshore wind power activities.

The Dividend yield was close to 5%.

I liked what I saw.

I purchased 1,350 shares in EDP, resulting in a cost of €5,063.

The EDP share price rose **by 29%** to a pre-Covid high of €4.81, and at that time, the shareholding was sitting on an **Unrealized Gain of €1,431.**

Keep up the good work!

Summary of the Performance in Utilities Companies:

National Grid	Unrealized Gain	5,448
SSE	Realized loss	-1,489
Centrica	Realized loss	-2,435
Enbridge	Unrealized Gain	606
Greencoat Renewables	Unrealized Gain	221
Energias de Portugal (EDP)	Unrealized Gain	1,431

At their pre-Covid highs, Utilities Companies generated overall net Realized and Unrealized Gains of €3,782, which more than protected the original sums invested from the ravages of inflation.

The investment in National Grid saved the day!

The holdings in the UK Utilities SSE PLC and Centrica PLC were sold as the control of their earnings by the UK Regulator did not bode well for the sustainability of their Dividends.

The non-UK holdings were providing, just before the arrival of Covid, a very satisfactory overall Dividend yield on the original cost of 6.5%+.

So far, Defensive industries like Pharma and Utilities have proved to be strong and safe investments (overall) in turbulent times.

Consumers spend on Pharma and Utilities in good times and bad.

So, are shares in the shops that sell products to the consumer considered to be Defensive in nature?

Let's find out.

Chapter Seven

Shopping for Security:

UK Retail Companies

"Yes I have everything for dinner"

Time to do some shopping in the Defensive Aisle!

Home Retail (UK)

Home Retail operated Argos, Homebase, and Habitat subsidiaries.

I was familiar with Argos, and I liked the brand as it provided low prices on a wide range of products. So, I was tempted to invest.

In September 2010, I bought 2,034 shares in Home Retail at a price of £2.30 each, which resulted in an all-in cost of €5,507.

How did the share price perform since the purchase?

Sep-10	£2.30
Sep-11	£1.26
Sep-12	£0.91
Sep-13	£1.68
Jun-14	£1.97

Pathetic.

Home Retail had slashed its 2012 Dividend, and I treat a Dividend cut as a warning signal.

It turned out that Home Retail were not a genuine Defensive stock because their customers engaged in consumer discretionary spending (not just the necessities).

Well, you live and learn!

In June 2014, I sold the entire holding in Home Retail generating proceeds of €4,917, realizing **a loss on the sale of -€590.**

Time to shop around for some real Defensive stocks: Grocery companies (Consumer Staples) should be a safe bet.

Morrisons Supermarkets

Morrisons, the UK's fourth-largest supermarket chain, were increasing investment in their Online channel, expanding their 'M local' convenience stores, and had recently started home deliveries.

Maybe Morrisons' shares would grow as their new strategies paid off.

In October 2013, the share had declined by 10% in the previous three months and was attractively priced.

The Dividend yield was also an attractive 4.3%.

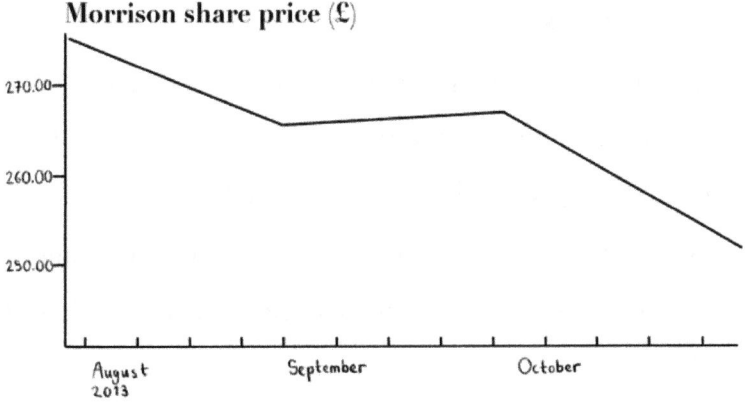

I purchased 955 Morrisons shares at a price of £2.66 per share in October 2013 at an all-in cost of €3,098.

Did the investment payoff?

The share price fell and fell, eventually reaching below £2.

These guys seemed to be unsuccessful in implementing the new approach, as quoted above.

I sold out in May 2015 for €2,552, at a price of £1.88 per share, incurring yet another loss on UK Retail shares of -€680.

I thought I had found a 'bargain investment' when I bought Morrisons shares.

Sometimes a lowly priced share is...er....just a lowly priced share!

But surely some Grocer is going to come out on top...once more into the breach!

Let's give another UK supermarket a go.

Sainsbury's

In 2016 Sainsbury's was the second largest supermarket chain in the United Kingdom, with a 16.9% share of the supermarket sector in the United Kingdom.

The company was split into three divisions: Sainsbury's Supermarkets (including convenience stores), Sainsbury's Bank, and Sainsbury's Argos.

Sainsbury's had earlier acquired Argos. Oh, Argos! We are back in again...a triumph of hope over experience!

Argos product lines were now available to Sainsbury's shoppers.

The Dividend yield was a satisfactory 4%+, and Dividend pay-outs were covered more than 2 times by profits:

The Sainsbury's share price was at a low point, and I saw it as a buying opportunity.

Maybe we have got a bargain here!

I purchased 1,930 ordinary shares in Sainsbury's at slightly above £2 in August 2016 and September 2016.

Additional charges brought the total cost of these purchases to €5,286.

I was becoming cautious in relation to shares in UK Retail companies, and Sainsbury's holding had reached a valuation of €6,000+ a year later in pre-covid February 2017.

I decided to clip my holdings and sold 330 shares in February 2017, at £2.66 each, generating a small profit of €98...*not enough to do a weekly shop!*

How did Sainsbury's share price perform after that sale?

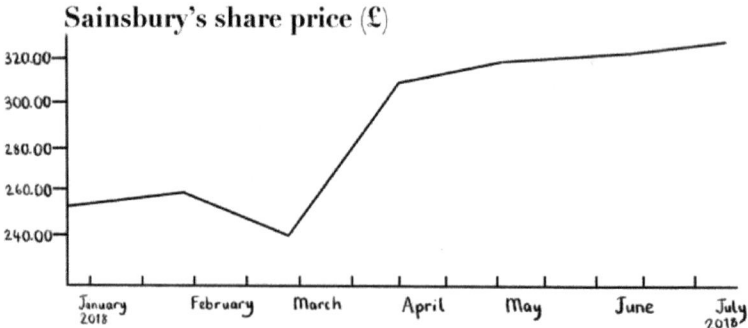

Sainsbury's share price (£)

In March 2018, the share price took off and jumped by 35%+.

Wow! My remaining shares were showing Unrealized Gains of €1,607.

What was going on?

Sainsbury's had agreed to buy Walmart's Asda for about £7.3 billion to create Britain's biggest supermarket group by market share. Sainsbury's could also roll out Argos in Asda stores."

My Unrealized Gains were dependent on the merger being cleared by the Competition and Markets Authority.

Then the deal was blocked by the Competition Authority, and the share price declined from £3+ down to under £2

I missed the boat...I should have sold!

My Unrealized Gains of €1,607 dwindled to just €20 at the supermarket's pre-Covid peak in December 2019.

Just enough for a nice bottle of red. I'll hang on in and pocket the 5.33% Dividends…!

Summary of the performance of UK Retail Companies:

Home Retail	Realized Loss	-€590
Morrisons Supermarkets	Realized Loss	-€680
Sainsbury's	Realized Gain	€98
Sainsbury's	Unrealized Gain	€20

The performance of the UK Retail shareholdings was unsatisfactory, generating an overall net loss of -€1,152 pre-Covid.

"Some things in life are bad

They can really make you mad

Other things just make you swear and curse."

Thanks for your good wishes, Monty Python!

However, Sainsbury's was paying Dividends of 5.33% on Cost.

I decided to hold on to them for the time being and pocket the Dividends.

So, what went wrong in the apparently reliable Defensive sector of 'Consumer Staples'?

Strategic challenges

Some companies faced difficult strategic challenges, and their share price performances were disappointing as a result.

Retail chain stores were experiencing reduced footfall as many shoppers had generally turned to the Internet for their purchases.

This meant the companies had to incur the cost of providing physical retail shops, *and in addition,* they now had to maintain eCommerce shopping channels.

This trend was later exacerbated during the many Covid lockdowns, making an already challenging environment even more difficult for this sector.

Will they make a comeback?

More on this topic later in the book.

Chapter Eight

Calling for Certainty:

Telecoms Companies

"Stop barking I'm on the phone"

Another Defensive sector is the **Telecoms Sector**.

Hardly anybody can do without their mobile cell phones these days!

But it is certainly a sector facing strategic challenges.

The Telecoms industry has changed over the last 30 years from landlines to mobile phones incorporating internet services.

Mobile data/Internet services have moved from 3G to 5G technology.

Telecom companies must spend large to keep up to date.

Many companies are broadening their offerings and providing streaming services, with some even generating their own content too.

These strategic challenges put pressure on Dividends and debt levels at Telecoms Companies.

Nevertheless, everyone seems to use a mobile phone these days. Let's give it a whirl.

AT&T

AT&T Inc. is the world's largest telecommunications company, the second-largest provider of mobile telephone services, and the largest provider of fixed telephone services in the United States.

AT&T was oftentimes considered to be one of the 'widows and orphan stocks' paying high and stable Dividends with low risks.

The company recently became the parent company of mass media conglomerate Warner Media, making it the world's largest media and entertainment company in terms of revenue.

This is certainly a company trying to diversify its revenue streams.

The share price was declining steadily towards the end of 2013:

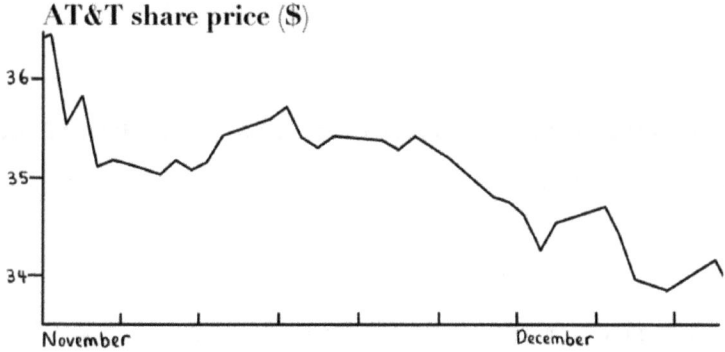

The Dividend Yield of 5.25% was attractive, and the US Dollar was weak. One Euro bought $1.3814 compared to $1.2105 in July 2012.

The weak dollar offered an opportunity to invest in *Amerikay* at very attractive Euro prices.

Euro US Dollar Exchange Rate

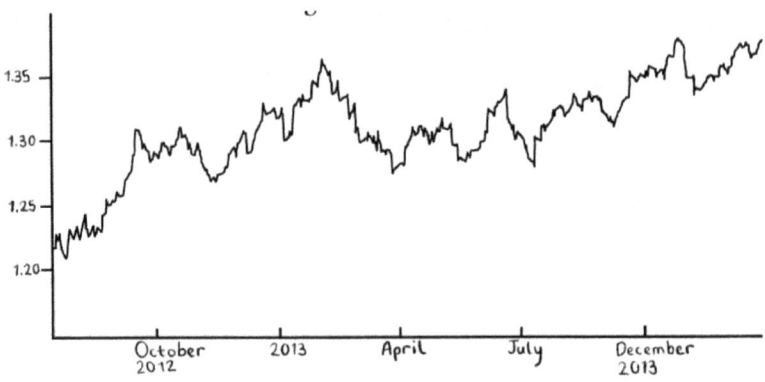

Will AT&T succeed in their strategy? Let's give them a go...

I purchased 145 shares in AT&T for €3,738 in December 2013.

How did things go since the purchase?

The share price rose from its purchase price of $34.52 to a pre-covid high of $39.08.

The valuation was further boosted by the strengthening in the US Dollar, which resulted in a very satisfactory net overall Unrealized Gain of €1,375, equivalent to 35%+.

Plus……. the Dividend yield continued to be very attractive at 5.44%+.

So far, so good!

Were there any European Telecoms companies similarly worth a flutter?

Telefónica

Telefónica SA is a Spanish multinational broadband and telecommunications provider with operations in Europe, Asia, and North, Central, and South America.

It is one of the largest telephone operators and mobile network providers in the world.

The company had scale and an attractive Dividend yield of 4.6%.

The share price was relatively stable in May 2015.

415 shares were bought in May 2015 at €14 each with an all-in cost of €5,482.

What happened to the Telefonica share price since the purchase?

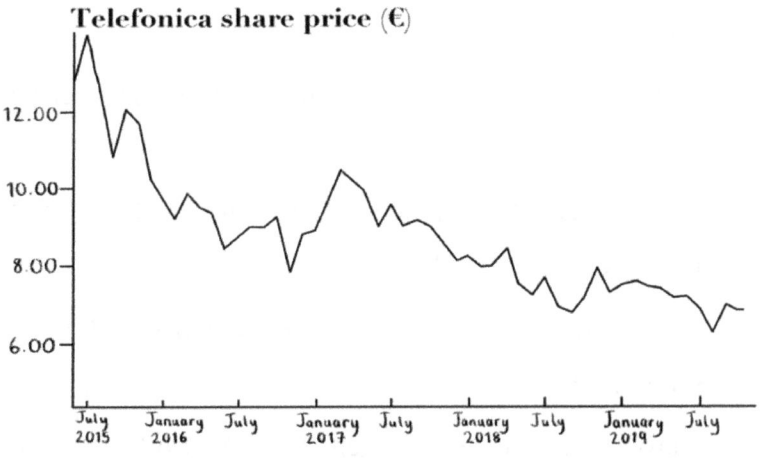

The share price almost halved ...a sorry situation!

Telefónica had also announced a cut in its 2016 Dividend from €0.75 to €0.55 cents a share.

I had missed the adverse news flow in 2016!

The company had unsustainable debt levels and was in danger of being downgraded by the Rating Agencies.

Maybe my internet signal was not working...ha de ha!

I offloaded the Telefonica holding on 15th October 2019 at a price of €7.04, realizing losses of -€2,603.

Was this a wise move?

The share price declined by a further 35% to €4.50 by the start of 2020.

I was lucky I took my losses on the chin!

I think I'll head back across the Atlantic Ocean, where the US Telecom companies seem to be faring better.

Verizon

Verizon is the second-largest major US wireless service provider.

They managed to maintain a Dividend yield above 4% for the better part of the last decade.

112 Verizon shares were bought in March 2018 at a cost of €4,385.

Euros were not exchanged for US Dollars as the exchange rate was unfavourable. This purchase was financed with the sale of Wells Fargo shares, a US dollar share, so no currency conversion was needed.

Has the Verizon purchase been successful?

Verizon shares rose strongly and, by December 2019, were valued at €6,205.

The Verizon shareholding was sitting on a welcome Unrealized Gain of €1,821.

Summary of the performance of Telecom Companies

Telefonica	Realized Losses	-€2,603
AT&T	Unrealized Gain	€1,375
Verizon	Unrealized Gain	€1,821

The Telecoms shareholdings provided a slight overall gain of €593.

The performance had suffered greatly from the investment in Telefonica.

The US Telecom companies saved the day.

Both US companies had made timely investments in the new 5G technologies, but the European company, Telefonica, was a laggard.

Companies that face strategic challenges have a bright future if they deal with the issues quickly, like AT&T and Verizon.

Chapter Nine
Identifying Your Needs:
Growth v Value Stocks

"Which remote is Netflix?"

In the previous chapters, we have covered how certain kinds of shares perform well in the 'good times' while others fare best in 'bad times.'

But there is another very important consideration when it comes to choosing a share: What kind of return do you want from your money?

As the reader knows, when you buy shares in a particular company and hold them for a length of time, the money you get as a reward for your investment has two parts:

The first part consists of the Dividends that any company pays you each year while you are holding the shares.

The second part is your capital gain, namely, the difference between the (higher) price you receive when you sell your holding and the (lower) price you paid when you made your investment.

All stocks fall broadly into three categories: Growth, Value, and Dividend shares.

Growth, Value, and Dividend stocks differ in the kind of return that an investor could expect from investing in this category of share.

Let me explain.

Growth Stocks

Growth stocks have substantially higher growth rates than the market average.

But they usually pay out very little by way of Dividends, if anything at all.

Growth companies invest their profits back into the company to fuel further growth.

A Growth investor assumes that the increases in share price will more than compensate for the loss of Dividend income.

It's an arrangement that suits many investors as, in several countries, the tax levied on Dividend income is higher than that levied on capital gains arising from selling the shares.

FAANG stocks [Facebook, Apple, Amazon, Netflix, Google] are examples of well-known Growth stocks.

These shares, historically, would be expected to grow more strongly than the rest of the market.

Growth Investors are hoping for large capital gains in relatively short periods of time. They believe a company has share price growth momentum.

Growth stocks are suited to young people who are earning salaries and are less dependent on income from their investments for day-to-day living.

Value Stocks

Value Stocks tend to be long-standing, reputable companies that are not expected to generate extraordinary increases in future profits.

They are the 'steady Eddies' of the stock market, generating gentle increases in stock prices and providing good Dividends annually.

The proven track record of the company should see the share price make steady gains over the years ahead. **They are called 'Value Stocks' because they are usually bought when the share is relatively cheap, i.e., they are good value.**

Value stocks are suited to investors who want to avoid large negative surprises, though unanticipated large positive or negative surprises can occasionally arise.

Value shares suit long-term investors because they can buy a well-regarded share at a relatively cheap valuation and hold it long-term.

Dividend stocks

Value stocks will often appeal to Investors who are focused on Dividends, as they usually pay good Dividends to attract investors.

Dividend Investors are looking for a well-regarded and stable stock that will deposit a generous Dividend regularly into their bank account.

These investors want some money on a regular basis.

These investors might include retirees who are seeking a replacement for their lost wages and salaries.

You don't need to dip into the kids' inheritance to pay for the annual cruises!

How can I tell if a share is a Growth, Value, or Dividend share?

Price Earnings Ratio (P/E Ratio)

Investopedia.com explains the P/E Ratio:

"The P/E ratio is a common tool for deciding whether a share is undervalued (Value) or overvalued (Growth).

The price-earnings ratio measures a share's current share price relative to its earnings per share (EPS)."

If the share price is $100 and the earnings attributable to each share are $10, then the P/E Ratio is 10 times.

Example

An investor is willing to pay 10 times the annual earnings of a share to buy the share. If he/she is willing to pay 20 times the annual earnings, the share would be much more highly priced.

P/E may be estimated on a trailing (backward-looking) or forward (projected) basis.

P/E ratios are used by investors and analysts to determine the relative value of a company's shares.

You take the Price Earnings Ratio (P/E Ratio) of the company you are interested in and directly compare it to the average P/E Ratio in its industry or on the market where you buy it.

119

Shares with a P/E Ratio higher than the average for their industry or stock exchange are considered to be expensive to buy (likely a Growth stock).

Shares with a P/E Ratio less than the market or sector average are considered to be undervalued (likely to be a Value stock).

The P/E Ratio is freely available in business newspapers and websites.

For example, in 2010, the average P/E Ratio for the London stock market was around 13 or 14 times.

Was there a good share in 2010 that had a P/E Ratio under the average, which would be tempting?

I looked at a report in 2010 (sourced by asking Google to give me the answer), showing shares with below-average P/E Ratios quoted on the London Stock Market.

The Aviva P/E Ratio, at 10 times in 2010, was significantly below the market average of 13/14 times.

Also, the Aviva Dividend Yield was relatively high at 5%+ in 2010, and therefore the share should generate value for the purchaser. This made Aviva both a Value share and a Dividend share.

Growth Stocks

On the other hand, a *high* P/E Ratio compared to the market average indicates the share is expensive to buy.

This usually means that market participants are expecting rapid growth in future earnings (i.e., it's considered to be a Growth stock) compared to those stocks with a slower growth forecast (Value stocks).

Microsoft

A good example of a Growth stock is Microsoft. Its P/E Ratio is 30 compared to 21.14 for the S&P 500. Its Dividend yield in August 2022 was 0.85%.

In the past five years, the share price has grown from $74.41 to $343.11.

Microsoft was a huge missed opportunity.

Why didn't I invest in Microsoft?

Well, one reason is most Growth Stocks are heavily dependent on the latest internet/social media technologies.

The older you are, the more difficult it is to understand these modern companies.

I love watching Netflix – also a Growth stock, by the way – but I can never figure out how to find it on the TV.

At my age, it is true that any device that requires two remote controls for access is way beyond my comprehension!

Are there any grandchildren in the house that can switch the darn thing on for me?

The main reason I don't do Growth Stocks is because, as a retiree, I am primarily seeking Dividend income to top up my pension.

Excuses, excuses!

Chapter Ten
Dividend Chasing: Insurance Companies

"Come back with my dividends"

I am retired, living on a pension, and my personal goal is to generate additional income from Dividends to support my lifestyle.

My approach to investing has the 'racy' nickname of being a 'Dividend Chaser.'

Therefore, stocks that appeal to me are stocks that pay out a high Dividend to shareholders, which can top up my employment and State pensions regularly.

Finding a Dividend Stock

We identify a Dividend stock by looking at its Dividend Yield.

As mentioned previously: *Total Annual Dividends per share divided by the Market Price of a share gives us a company's Dividend yield.*

Like: Interest paid on a bank deposit divided by the amount of the deposit is how we can calculate the Bank Deposit Rate.

Well-regarded stocks with Dividend yields of 4%, 5%, and even 6% clearly signal that the stock is a Dividend stock.

Dividend Investors need to be wary of stocks that pay out extremely high Dividends. Any yields above 6% could be risky as companies may be paying out more than they can afford.

You can easily check if a company's Dividend yield is sustainable by googling the company's **"Pay-out ratio,"** which is the % of profits paid out to shareholders in Dividends each year.

As a rule of thumb, companies should generally pay out no more than 50% of profits. It's usually a bad sign if they pay out more.

For example, in 2019, the Dividend yield on **Royal Mail** stock was a very attractive 10.83%, but the Pay-out ratio was 80%.

Inevitably, the Dividend was cut by 70% in 2020 as the company retained more of its profits to support investment in its business.

Wouldn't you have been disappointed if you had invested in **Royal Mail** stock in 2019 for the 'good Dividends'?

Insurance sector.

The insurance sector is well known to be a reliable payer of Dividends to shareholders.

This is because, as many of us are probably painfully aware, insurance companies tend to pass on any losses, ultimately, to their customers.

An informal industry standard has developed whereby these companies pay generous Dividends to shareholders.

Any company that deviates from this industry norm tends not to attract investors.

As a Dividend investor, I decided to 'insure' my annual income by making investments in this sector.

Geddit? Ah, never mind!

Understanding the Sector

There are three kinds of insurance companies: Life and Pensions, General Insurance, and Reinsurance companies.

All these insurance companies theoretically make money in two ways:

1. By charging enough premiums to cover the expected accidental losses that they must cover (plus an underwriting margin)

2. By earning investment returns on "the float" caused by the excess premiums, they are left with after paying out losses. Also, the float is augmented by the long delays before customers are recompensed for the losses which they have insured.

In 2010, I decided to get involved in the Insurance Sector.

I started with Aviva.

Aviva is a British multinational insurance company headquartered in London, England. It has about 33 million customers across 16 countries.

In the United Kingdom, Aviva is the largest UK general insurer and a leading Life and Pension provider.

I looked at a report in 2010 showing Aviva shares with a Dividend Yield of 5%+ which enkindled my interest in the share.

The Aviva P/E Ratio, at 10 times, was also relatively modest, and therefore the share was attractively priced.

In July 2010, 530 shares were purchased in Aviva, resulting in an all-in cost of €2,131. (Price £3.26)

In April 2012, I bought an additional 674 shares in Aviva at an all-in cost of €2,589. (Price £3.06)

How did the Aviva share perform since the purchases?

Splendidly... up 25%

This shareholding was generating Unrealized capital gains of €1,175, calculated at its pre-Covid peak price in February 2020.

The Dividend yield had reached 7%+ by then, and the Pay-out ratio was only 52% (meaning they were paying out little more than half the profits.

Jolly good show…more Insurance, please!

Munich RE

Munich Re is a *Reinsurance* company that insures the insurers.

It re-insures a portion of the risk covered by its clients (insurance companies) worldwide.

Munich Re provides cover for life, health, casualty, transport, aviation, space, fire, and engineering activities.

The Dividend yield at purchase was an attractive 4.45%, and the Dividend pay-out ratio was an undemanding 40%.

The P/E Ratio was a modest 8 times: The share had Value.

In December 2013, 30 shares were bought in Munich Re at €159.25 per share and an all-in cost of €4,831.

How did the share price perform since the purchase?

The share price shot up…. **and I sold 11 shares in January 2020 at a price of €264.70, realizing a profit of €1,053.**

A value share….? Most definitely, yes!

A month later, I was sitting on an Unrealized Gain of €2,000 based on the share's pre-Covid high.

My combined Realized and Unrealized Gains from this investment amounted to €3,053 yielding a 70% return since my purchase in December 2013.

More insurance stocks, please!

In Switzerland, the Swiss stock market (SMI) was rising strongly in January 2014.

Zurich Insurance

Zurich employs 53,000 employees, and it provides a wide range of property, casualty, and life insurance products and services in more than 210 countries and territories.

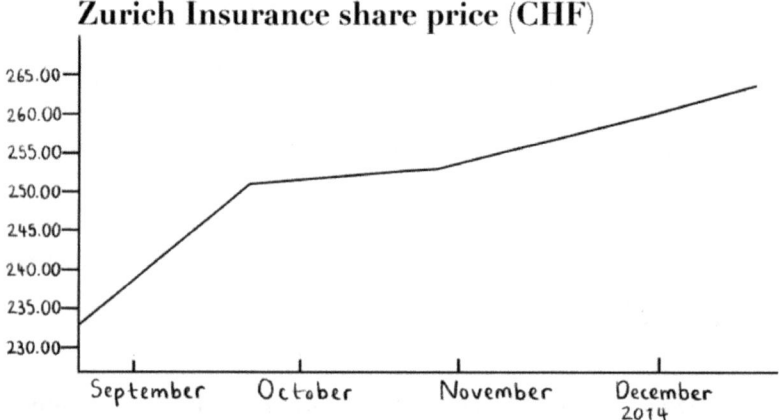

Zurich's Dividend yield was 6%+, and the P/E Ratio was only 10.

The movement in the share price in January 2014 was upward.

In December 2014, 30 shares were bought in Zurich Insurance at CHF257.40 per share and an all-in cost of €6,388.

How did the Zurich share price perform since the purchase?

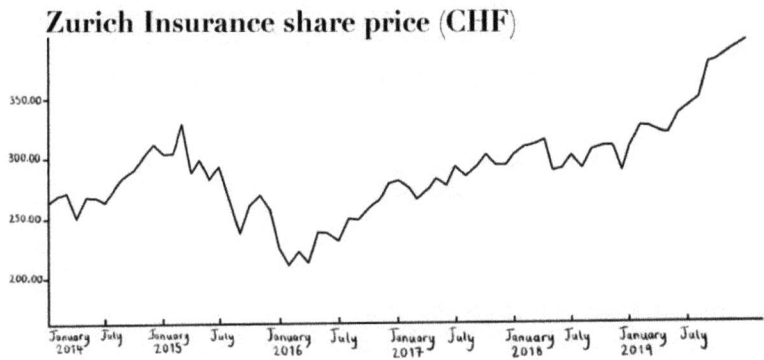

The share initially fell dramatically, in 2015, from its purchase price of CHF257.40 but subsequently performed gloriously.

Keep cool, man.... keep cool!

These shares were generating Unrealized Gains of €4,688, based on the pre-Covid February 2020 peak price.

Yodelayeeoh!

How about a French Insurance Company?

Axa

Axa is one of the world's leading insurance and asset management groups, serving 105 million clients in 54 countries.

Axa works across three major business lines: property-casualty insurance, life & savings, and asset management.

The Axa share price was strongly rising in 2015.

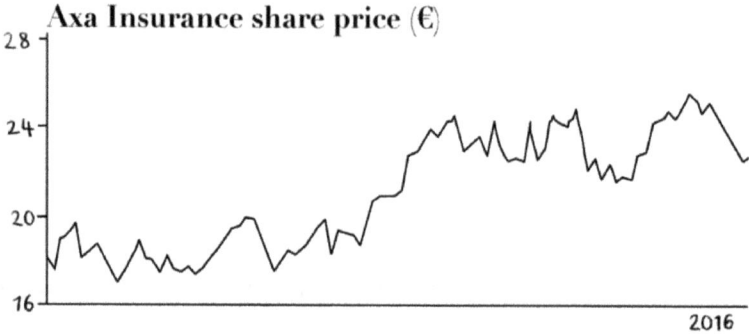

The Dividend yield was c.4%, and its P/E Ratio was acceptable at 10 times.

In the Investor section on its website, AXA said it aimed at increasing earnings per share by 3-7% annually in 2016-2020.

I'll have a bit o' that!

In April 2015, 225 shares in Axa were bought at an all-in cost of €5,215. The share price was €22.82, and the dividend yield was well above 3.5%.

What happened next?

The share price peaked in early 2018 at €26.86 and then fell below €20.

I didn't panic but held on to the dividends.

And by December 2019, the Axa share had risen to €25.11, so the shareholding was 8% ahead, at its pre-Covid peak price, **experiencing €434 of Unrealized Gains.**

Axa meets my objectives of good Dividends and a gentle increase in its share price.

Vive La France!

Where to next? Maybe back to Germany? Any more German insurers?

Allianz

Allianz is the market leader in German Insurance and has 150,000 employees in 70 countries serving 100 million customers worldwide.

Its Dividend yield of 4.22% was the fifth highest in the Frankfurt, Germany, stock market (DAX 30).

Its Pay-out ratio was only 53%, so the Dividend was sustainable.

At the time, the Price Earnings Ratio for the top 30 shares quoted on the German stock market (DAX) was c.15 times.

Allianz Insurance had a P/E Ratio of only 11.3 times.

So, Allianz was trading relatively cheaply compared to the market and could be classified as a Value share.

Don't look a gift horse in the mouth!

In January 2016, 42 shares were bought in Allianz SE at an all-in cost of €6,557.

How did the Allianz share perform since the purchase?

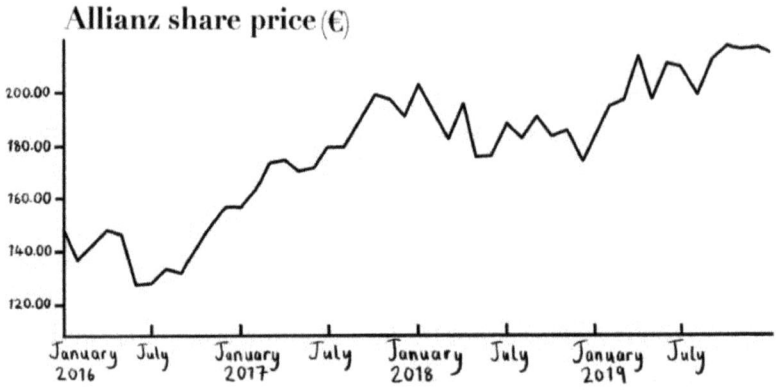

Upwards and upwards……

I was sitting on Unrealized Gains of €3,187, measured at its pre-Covid peak price, together with a healthy stream of Dividends.

Seems you can't go wrong buying insurance shares.

Swiss Re

The Swiss Re Group is a leading provider of *Reinsurance.*

In January 2018, 65 shares were bought in Swiss Re at CHF91.30 per share and an all-in cost of €5,158.

Was the performance a good one?

The Swiss RE 2017 Letter to shareholders reported that 2017 was a turbulent year in which insurers saw their accounts hit by no fewer than three hurricanes in the North Atlantic, two earthquakes in Mexico, two large forest fires in California, and storms in Australia.

The report also stated that History showed that loss concentrations of this kind occur every five to seven years. Premiums were subsequently increased in the wake of a year such as 2017.

Re-insurers usually raise premiums when losses arise, passing the losses to their customers and insulating their shareholders.

Swiss Re increased Dividends by 3% in spite of the 2017 losses.

How did the Swiss Re share price perform since the purchase?

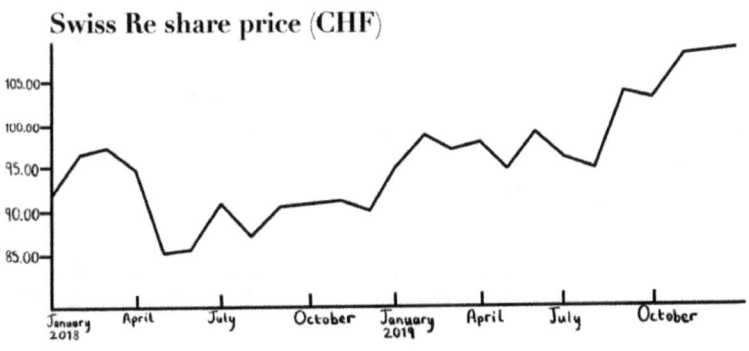

Swiss Re share price (CHF)

Swiss Re shares had generated Unrealized Gains of €1,753, based on the Pre-Covid peak price.

I became brave and took on a new country.

Goodness gracious me!......Peter Sellars

Generali

Assicurazioni Generali S.p.A. (Generali) is the largest Insurance company in Italy and the third largest in the world.

Generali had just issued impressive results.

The share was trading relatively cheaply with a P/E Ratio of less than 10 and a Dividend yield of 5.63%.

Oftentimes, investors are wary of Italy due to its political risks and unstable governments, but Italy has survived these problems before.

Aw heck, jump in and get a bit of excitement!

In August 2018, I bought 350 shares at an all-in cost of €5,281.

How has the Generali share price performed?

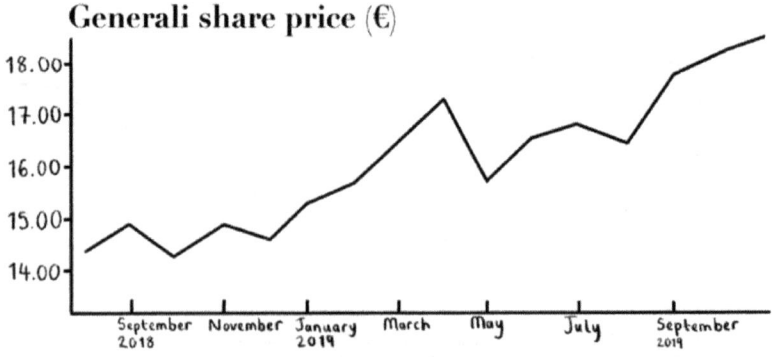

Generali share price (€)

At the pre-Covid peak price, the shares had generated Unrealized Gains of €1,205, up 20%+ in a little over 1 year.

...*Wow!*

Time to venture once again into the Netherlands?

Aegon

Aegon is a Dutch multinational life insurance, pensions, and asset management company.

In 2020 Aegon employed approximately 26,000 people worldwide, serving millions of customers.

The Aegon Dividend yield was over 6.5%, and the P/E Ratio was only 6 times:

This was a share clearly attractive to both Value and Dividend Investors.

In October 2018, 500 shares in Aegon were bought at €5.27 each, at an all-in cost of €2,677.

How did the Aegon share price perform?

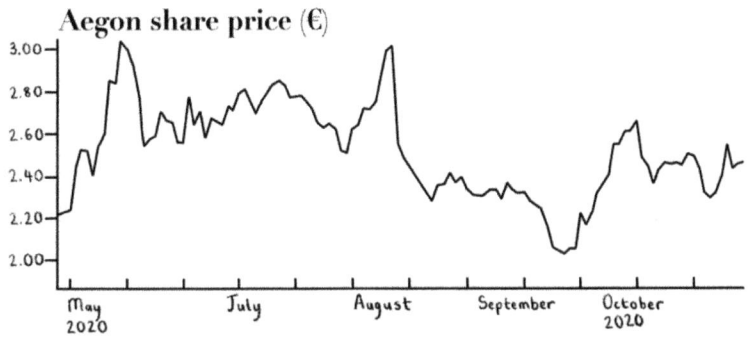

Aegon share price (€)

Down and down to a pre-Covid 'peak price' of €4.07…….. the rotters!

At that time, the Unrealized Loss was -€642.

What on earth had happened?

Aegon's US business reported a bigger-than-expected fall in underlying pre-tax profit for the second half of 2019.

This bad news caused the decline in the Aegon share price.

Maybe another Dutch insurer, not heavily involved in the USA, might help the cause.

Surely the Dutch won't let me down again?

NN Group

NN Group is one of the largest insurance and asset management companies in the Netherlands.

The NN Group share price was trading at a relatively low €38.

The Dividend yield was 4.89%, and the P/E Ratio was just over 10.

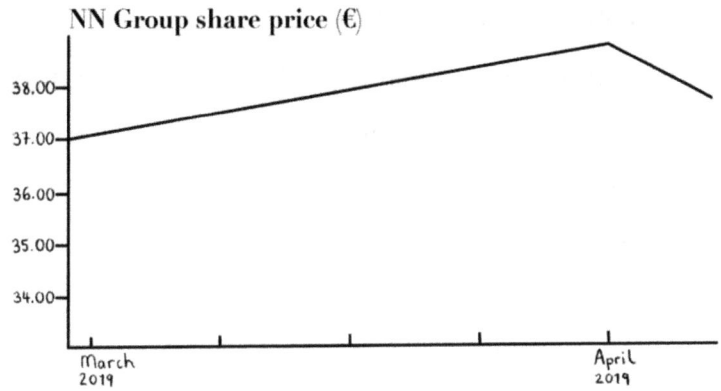

In April 2019, 140 shares in NN Group were purchased at an all-in cost of €5,420.

Hopefully, Holland would deliver the goodies this time.

How did the NN Group share price perform?

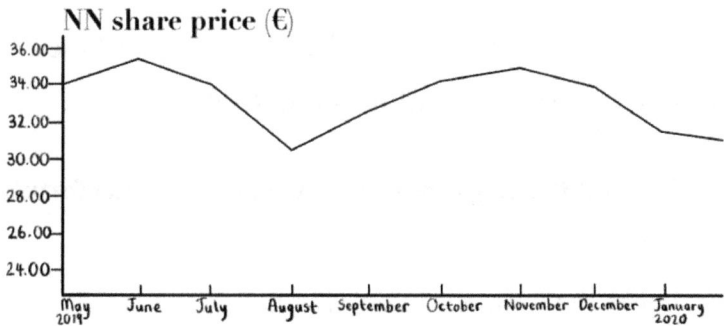

The decline in the NN share price to €32 generated a pre-Covid Unrealized Loss of -€542, down by 10%.

Twice bitten by the Dutch…not shy enough!

The next move was across the North Sea. Ah, go on, give Boris a chance!

Legal & General Insurance

The UK's top life insurer, Legal & General Group, had a modest P/E Ratio of 8.04 (compared to the market average of 15.85) and a good Dividend yield of 6.6% (compared to the market average of 3.41%).

A keen purchase for Dividend Investors…

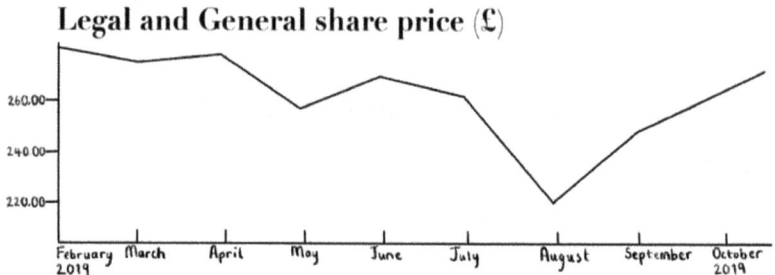

The share price was on a sharp upward trajectory.

In October 2019, 1,800 shares were purchased in Legal & General at an all-in cost of €5,533.

How did the Legal & General share price perform?

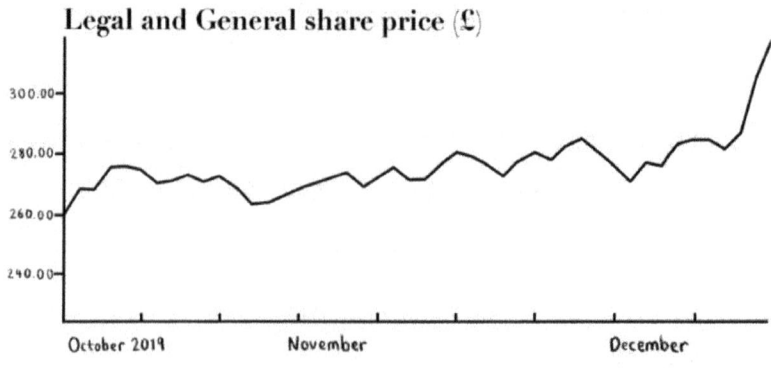

Jolly good show!

Unrealized Gains were €1,282 at L&G's pre-Covid peak price.

Pre-Covid Summary of Insurance Shareholdings Performance:

Aviva	Unrealized Gain	1,175
Munich Re	Realized gain	1,053
Munich Re	Unrealized Gain	2,000
Zurich Insurance	Unrealized Gain	4,688
Axa	Unrealized Gain	435
Allianz	Unrealized Gain	3,187
Swiss Re	Unrealized Gain	1,753
Generali	Unrealized Gain	1,205
Aegon	Unrealized Loss	-642
NN group	Unrealized Loss	-542
Legal & General	Unrealized Gain	1,282

Overall Capital gains were €15,594.

The Dividend yield (on original cost) was an average of 6.45% which was a great encouragement to hold on to these Insurance shares.

INSURANCE............ IN SURELY!

Outlook for Insurance Companies

The bulk of European Insurance Risk is taken by the small number of large re-insurers in Europe at a price determined by them. Large re-insurers demand higher prices from their customers (the ordinary Insurance Companies) as losses increase. This forces local insurers to charge policyholders more.

Local politicians are demanding that customers (their voters) should not be ripped off by insurance companies.

But Insurance Companies must recoup the higher prices set by the Reinsurers or shoulder the insurance risks themselves.

The politicians have not yet given up..........vigilance is called for when investing in this sector.

But, so far, so good!

Chapter Eleven

Shop Local:

Selected Irish Small Cap Companies

"I like to shop local"

Investors often forget to value their own knowledge and experience when it comes to selecting stocks to invest in.

My brother worked in medicine his whole life. Yet when it came to investing, he was more interested in South American gold mines than medical companies in which he would have had considerable expertise.

His portfolio suffered because he invested in what he didn't understand.

For this reason, I advocate a 'shop local' approach. If you are familiar with small local companies, then you may know more about their prospects than traders on 'Wall Street.'

Being an Irishman, I had familiarity with smaller Irish companies that would not attract attention from international analysts.

This meant I had an edge when investing as I could draw on local knowledge.

Shares in small companies are inherently riskier than those of large companies because they are usually not well diversified in their products or their geographies .... yet.

But I felt I could give them a go, armed with my local Irish knowledge.

As we know, the Irish stock market fell dramatically due to the financial crash but from 2009 onwards, the Irish stock market powered ahead.

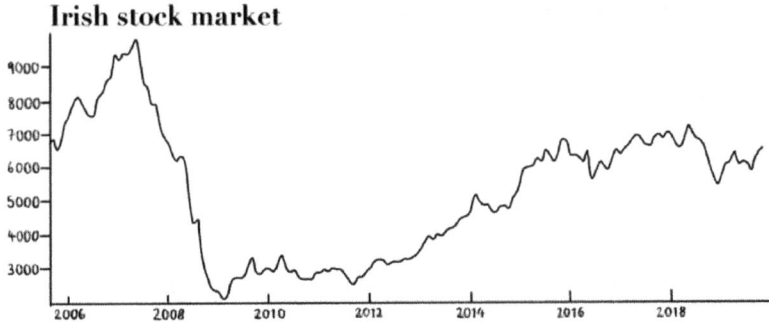

Irish stock market

The Irish stock market had doubled in value since the Financial Crisis.

A Small Cap Company

Market Capitalization is a measure of company size calculated by multiplying the number of shares issued by a company by the market price of one share.

In stock market terms, a small cap company, in an Irish context, has a market cap of anywhere between €300m and €2bn.

In contrast, in 2010, building materials company **CRH plc** had a market cap of €10bn+, making it the largest market cap quoted in the Irish stock market.

Small companies have the capacity to grow sharply, thereby increasing the share price rapidly…but they can also collapse more quickly!

Between 2010–2012, I decided to 'shop local' and buy companies that had small market capitalizations (Small Caps) on the Irish stock market.

Would my approach pay off?

Greencore

I remember the cheese of my childhood,

and the bread that we cut with a knife.

When the children helped with the housework,

and the men went to work, not the wife.

The bread and cheese never needed a fridge.

I remember the milk from the bottle,

with the yummy cream on the top.

Our dinner came hot from the oven

and not from the fridge in the shop!

(Source unknown)

Greencore provides the food for the fridge in the shop!

Greencore Group plc is an international manufacturer of convenience foods.

They supply a wide range of chilled, frozen, and ambient foods to some of the most successful retail and food service providers in Ireland, the UK, and the US.

This Irish share is quoted on the London stock exchange.

Greencore's market capitalization was €1bn during 2010.

This made it a very small company in Irish stock market terms.

When investing in small companies, I like to do my homework so I can feel confident in making a purchase.

Let's look at the fundamentals.

Greencore is classified as a Consumer Defensive stock and therefore is not overly sensitive to ups and downs in the economic cycles.

A man's gotta eat when a man's gotta eat!

The company provided readymade food to the growing number of families where both parents are working and have little time for food preparation.

Greencore was involved in a business sector that was experiencing high levels of growth.

Greencore also was expanding internationally – particularly into the United States – thereby facilitating growing revenues as the company gained access to wider markets.

Financial Performance

I found some surprising, good news when looking in the investor section on its website:

"Our business is performing very strongly with operating profits up 43%, EPS up 15%, debt down by 42%, and a positive outlook for the rest of the year".

Checking the share price quickly on the Irish stock exchange, I saw that Greencore shares had closed *2.8% lower* at €1.22 in Dublin.

There seemed to be a disconnect between the company's financial performance and the trend in the share price. The share was clearly unloved by the Financial Analysts.

For me, the share seemed to be a bargain.

The first purchase

I purchased a holding of 1,510 ordinary shares for €2,002 in June 2010, which included the standard additional charges of €50 commission (two separate trades) and stamp duty of €19.32.

I kept an eye on things in the following months, and lo and behold:

Again, from the investor section on its website:

"We are delighted to have delivered 7.9% sales growth for the first half of 2011 and to have driven this through to a 42% growth in continuing adjusted earnings per share.

We remain optimistic about our ability to drive growth and shareholder value from both our existing business and from corporate development in the months and years ahead."

The disconnect between the positive trend in profits and the poor performance in the share price continued.

The logic for a second purchase was even more compelling!

I took up my "rights entitlements" for Greencore in August 2011 when a holding of 1,258 ordinary shares was purchased for €579.

A 'rights entitlement' is when shares are offered by the company to its existing shareholders at a deep discount.

After the second purchase, the accumulated holdings were 2,768 at an all-in cost of €2,581.

How did the share price perform?

The share price rose to £2+...... *very satisfactory indeed!*

Financial Analysts in places like London noticed the growth in profits and began to recommend the stock.

Welcome on board, guys!

Who are the Financial Analysts?

These are the people who track the fortunes of quoted companies for their clients.

They can often be portrayed as fellows wearing red braces!

What now to do?

The problem that faces the small investor is that he will not sell if the share price has increased in value as he is afraid that he might lose out on further profits.

Similarly, the small investor usually doesn't sell if the price falls as he fears that doing so crystallizes his losses forever.

The consequences are that **the small Investor rarely sells**.

In 2014, the Greencore Dividend yield was a lowly 2%, and the market value of the holding had increased by more than €5,000

The Dividend Yield target for my portfolio had been set between 3.5% - 6.5%.

Greencore's Dividend yield of 2% was not within my desired range.

As a Dividend Investor, it was time to take some money off the table and reinvest in a stock that paid out more attractive Dividends.

The first sale

The first sale occurred in June 2014, when 1,700 shares were sold, generating a profit of €4,450.

I continued to hold the remaining shares as I was enjoying the ride!

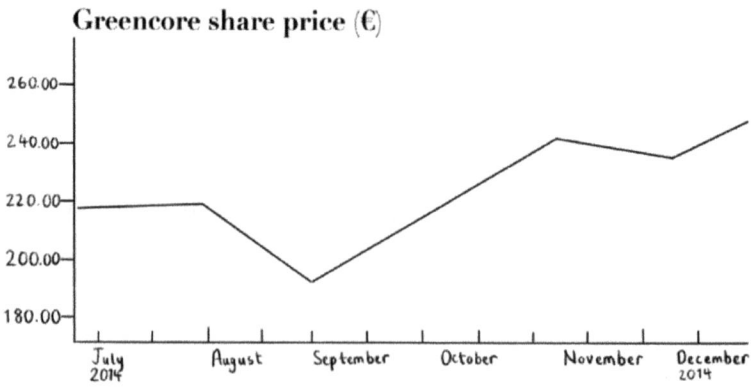

149

The share price rose between June 2014 and December 2015...yet the Dividend yield continued to be unattractive at a 2.5% level.

That led to the decision to sell the *remaining* holding and reinvest the proceeds in a share which would pay out a much higher Dividend.

The sale of the remaining holding of Greencore shares was executed in December 2015.

The profit generated on the second sale was €3,867, and the cumulative profit from both sales amounted to €8,317.

This profit compared very favorably with the original cash investment of €2,581.

Was it the right time to sell?

In the Summer of 2017, Peacock Foods, a key Greencore US subsidiary, lost a contract to supply Starbucks in the US.

Greencore was also forced to recall some other US product lines after failing a routine Food and Drugs Administration (FDA) inspection at its Rhode Island plant.

The Greencore US expansion - which had begun so strongly - had become a nightmare.

My sale of the shares in December 2015 at £3.31 per share compared favorably with their pre-Covid peak price in December 2019 of £2.68.

Luck was on our side. Or, as Napoleon is quoted as saying:

"The best generals are the lucky ones."

What other small cap Irish companies was I familiar with?

The sea, oh the sea, is the border to be.

Oh! Thank God we're surrounded by water.

(Brendan Behan)

Irish Continental Group (ICG)

Ireland is an island state, and it needs shipping to carry goods, cars, trucks, and passengers to and from the UK and France.

ICG is the major player in the provision of sea transport services for Ireland and the main conduit for Irish Goods that must use sea transport to reach their markets.

ICG also carries passengers and cars on sea routes between Ireland, the United Kingdom, and Continental Europe. It operates out of Dublin and Belfast.

ICG shares should float upwards... hee hee!

Let's look at the fundamentals.

In the Noughties, ICG had invested over €500 million in new vessels, port infrastructure, and acquisitions and became the leading Irish marine transport operator.

On a visit to the company's website, I spotted in their investor section that capital expenditure in 2009 was just €4.8 million. No new ships were needed, and net debt was reduced from €48.7 million at the start of the year to €21.7 million by year-end.

This meant that there might be no debt by the end of 2010. So, ICG would be able to operate for the foreseeable future with no bank repayments required.

With a market capitalization of €1.1bn, ICG was a small company in stock market terms.

Small is beautiful...

The first purchase

In January 2011, a holding of 1,390 ordinary shares was purchased at an all-in cost of €2,200.

In February 2012, a second holding of 1,600 ordinary shares was purchased in February 2012, at a slightly lower price than the earlier purchase.

The second investment had an all-in cost of €2,506.

The cumulative investment in Irish Continental Group (ICG Group) was now €4,706... *Quite enough committed for the time being!*

By the end of that year, ICG's cash-generating ability was being highlighted in Irish media sources.

One Irish Analyst went so far as to describe the listed ferry company as a "cash machine."

How did the share price perform afterward?

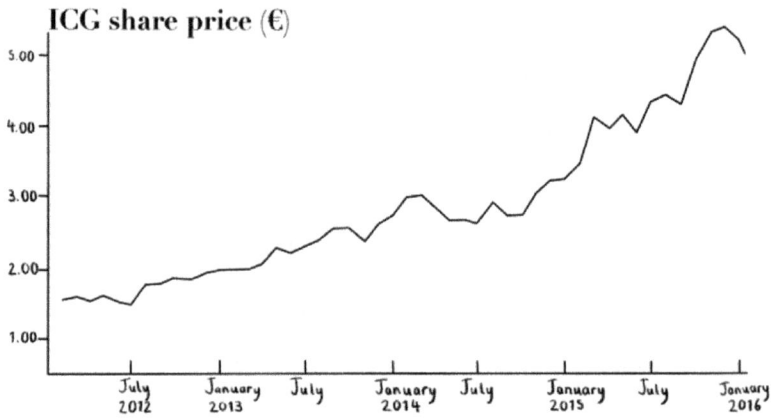

ICG share price (€)

My Shares in Irish Continental Group had more than doubled in value by May 2015 and were valued at more than €11,000 by that date.

It was now time to cash in some of the gains.

The first sale occurred in May 2015, when 1,225 shares were sold, generating profits of €3,269.

A further sale of 550 Irish Continental Group (ICG Group) shares took place in July 2015, which generated profits of €1,368.

As the 2015 2% Dividend yield was well below my minimum 3.5% target, I sold the remaining holding and began to look for higher Dividends elsewhere.

The sale of the remaining holding generated profits of €4,587.

Overall dealings in Irish Continental Group shares generated profits of €9,224...a net return of 196%.

I was clearly able to walk on water! Get it – water – ships - ah, forget it!

Summary of the performance of the Selected Irish Small Companies' shareholdings

Greencore	Realized Gains	€8,317
Irish Continental Group	Realized Gains	€9,224

An overall profit from dealings in these companies generated profits of €17,541.

You two little beauties...you!

I will continue to look at small cap Irish Companies' shares as I am a resident of Ireland and very familiar with the activities and market positioning of these companies.

As the Irish saying goes, 'Better the divil you know than the divil you don't know!'

I need to remind you that many Irish investors were wiped out during the Financial Crisis of 2008/9 due to the collapse in bank shares.

It was particularly acute for those who had most of their savings invested in the 'safety' of Bank shares.

Diversify........ Diversify........... Diversify!

The investment decisions taken in the next three Chapters encouraged me to add international stocks to my portfolio.

Why invest abroad? To achieve geographic diversification.

Different countries have different resource endowments, such as oil and natural gas, minerals, forests, arable land, rivers, educational systems, and so on. As a result, countries have different industrial compositions.

Countries may also have different economic regulations, including environmental regulations, rules governing trade unions, and different infrastructures.

In a large country or a political entity like the European Union, conditions may vary in different regions such as Northern Europe, Southern Europe, Western Europe, and Eastern Europe.

In modern economies, there is a constant restructuring of industries in response to changes in demand or new technologies that affect supply. It can be easier to adapt a portfolio to these changes by buying shares in different countries.

Currency Risk

There is often an additional complication when investing in international shares, namely, exchange rates. You may make a profit on an international share (in its home currency) that is wiped out by an adverse currency movement. Sometimes you may decide to delay selling the share until the exchange rate improves.

The next three chapters present my experience of investing in Germany (the largest economy in the European Union), the United States (the largest economy in the world), and the United Kingdom, a large economy with historical ties to Ireland.

I confine my attention to large companies because they can help me diversify industrially as well as internationally.

Also, it is easier to find information on large companies in my local press and English-speaking websites.

Chapter Twelve
Buying the Big Players:
Selected German Large Cap Companies

"German sausages are the wurst"

Many retail investors only invest in the country that they live in.

What happens if war, famine, earthquakes, or tsunamis might arise in your own country or the wrong sort of people get into political power?

Never say never!

How should one go about choosing overseas companies?

I began to search on the internet and examined companies that had Dividend yields between 3.5% and 6.5% with Pay-out ratios not exceeding 50%.

Tables, giving relevant information, can be sourced for the US, Canada, UK, Scandinavia, and other Western European stock markets.

I wondered about investing in a big player in Germany.

I asked Google what companies pay high Dividends in Germany:

High Dividend Yields <u>2022:</u>

Company	Dividend Yield %
BASF	8.50%
Allianz	4.62%
Munich Re	3.76%

I already had shares in the above companies...*unsurprising for a self-professed 'Dividend Chaser'!*

If a company does not pay good Dividends, I invest for the short-term only.

Let's take a few short-term punts on low Dividend companies.

Siemens

Siemens is a German conglomerate and the largest industrial manufacturing company in Europe.

Industry, Energy, Healthcare, and Infrastructure are its main activities.

Siemens employ approximately 372,000 people worldwide and reported global revenue of around €83 billion in 2017.

In 2011, the share price was trending sharply downwards:

The Economist reported:

"Alarm bells rang in the summer: new orders had dropped in almost every division, compared with a year earlier, most dramatically in energy, infrastructure, and cities (which includes high-speed trains). Orders within Germany and from India had fallen by over 40%. Even China ordered 11% less."

Analysts were predicting a Dividend Yield in 2018 of *3.80%,* supported by a moderate *pay-out ratio* of 44.47%...... *maybe have a go?*

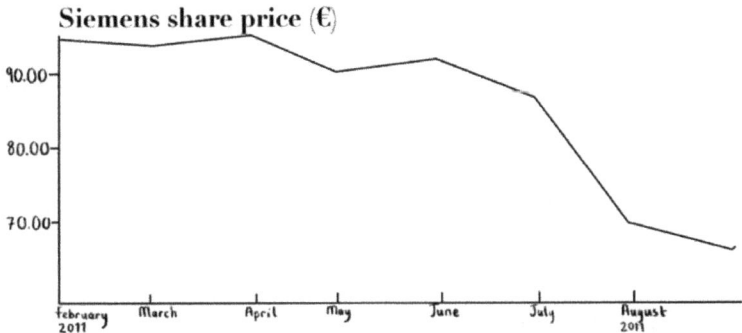

The share price was falling, and I purchased 46 shares in Siemens in August 2011 at an all-in cost of €3,333.

What happened after the purchase?

Osram Licht AG was spun off from parent firm Siemens in Summer 2013 and floated on the German stock market.

With this move, Osram, the world's largest pure-play lighting company, became an individual public company.

80% of Osram Licht's overall capital stock was allotted to existing Siemens shareholders at a ratio of 10:1 (i.e., the given shareholder received one new Osram share for every ten Siemens shares).

I received 5 shares, and in April 2015, I sold them at a profit of €208.

This holding was too small, so I turned it into cash…cash is king!

Meanwhile, the Siemens share price climbed steeply:

The share price rose from €71.29 in 2011 to almost €115 by December 2016.

The Dividend Yield was under 3%, so I decided to sell.

18 shares were sold at a price of €114.5 in December 2016, **realizing gains of €653.**

The remaining shares were sold in July 2017 at €116.02, **netting additional capital gains of €1,239.**

Overall, the dealings in Siemens (including the sale of my small Osram holding) generated a total profit of €2,100.

Wunderbar!

Let's give some German <u>software</u> engineers a go!

SAP

SAP is the world's third-largest software manufacturer.

It develops enterprise software for managing business operations and customer relations. It has 404,000 customers worldwide.

A big problem was the miserly 1% Dividend yield, but I understood that many Technology companies pay little or no Dividends.

If you want technology shares… poor Dividends… suck it up, baby!

I had experience in SAP products, and so, in Spring 2014, I decided to invest.

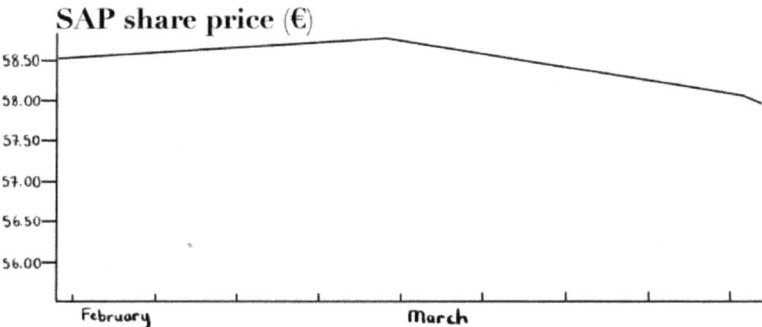

SAP share price (€)

The share was declining by the end of March 2014, having risen in the previous two months…*was this an opportunity to buy?*

92 shares were purchased in SAP, <u>for the short term,</u> in March 2014, when the price was trading at a relatively low €53.97, at an all-in cost of €5,020.

What happened to the SAP share price?

The share price had climbed to €78.81 by September 2016, but the Dividend yield remained low.

27 shares were sold that September and realized **a gain of €597.**

The share continued to climb! But Dividends remained miserly!

I sold a further 11 shares at €93.04 in May 2017, making an extra **€382.**

The remaining shares were sold in September 2019, generating **a gain of €1,837.**

Overall, the investment in SAP generated Realized Gains of €2,816.

Were the sales of SAP shares a smart move?

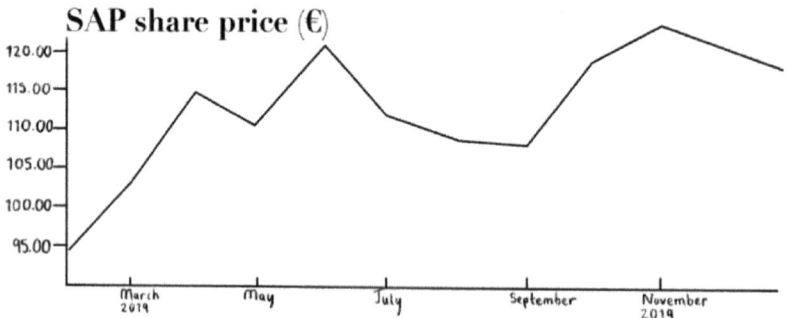

Certainly not!

The share's pre-Covid peak was above €115 versus the €89.55 sale price in 2019.

I slept easy in my own bed, but if I had sold SAP later, I could have afforded to sleep in Trump Tower in New York!

More German shares, please!

Deutsche Post

Deutsche Post owns the world's largest courier company (DHL).

In August 2017, 96 shares in Deutsche Post were bought at €32.80 per share, costing €3,200.

How did the share price perform since the purchase?

The share price continued to rise in 2017 but then declined significantly through 2018 and the early part of 2019.

Later in 2019, the share price showed some recovery but then leveled off.

I had had enough and cashed in my chips in November 2019, realizing a gain of €37.

Enough for a few beers at the Munich Oktoberfest!

Summary of the performance in Selected German Large Cap Companies:

Siemens	Realized gains	€2,100
SAP	Realized gains	€2,816
Deutsche Post	Realized Gains	€37

In overall terms, the Selected German Large Cap Companies generated net gains of €4,953.

...not a bad day's work!

Let's see if similar gains can be made by diversifying into the US of A...

Chapter Thirteen
Buying in a Safe Economy:
Selected US Large Cap Companies

"Let's invest in General Electric"

In 2008, when the market was reverberating from the shock of the Financial Crash, I decided to invest in large American companies with a long and prestigious pedigree.

General Electric (GE)

General Electric was the only company listed in the Dow Jones Industrial Average, (top 30 US industrial companies), when it was first calculated in 1896, and still qualified to be in the Dow Jones in 2008.

The Company's products and services ranged from aircraft engines, power generation, and oil and gas production equipment to medical imaging, financing, and industrial products.

At one point, GE's Market Capitalization had reached $102b.

...a very big gorilla, indeed.

In August 2008, I bought 250 shares in General Electric at $28.24 per share, costing €4,901.

How did the share price perform since the purchase?

The share price declined by almost 20%. The Dividend yield had dipped below 3%, and the share price performance was getting worse.

I sold the shares in 2017 when the price of the shares was below the purchase price, but due to the favorable

Euro Dollar exchange rate movement, I realized a Gain of €33.

Was I right to sell the GE shares?

You betcha!

Afterward, the share price fell to $5 compared to my $27.16 sale price.

Shocking... yeah, shocking... get it? They blew more than one fuse!

What happened at GE?

The company had gone into consumer lending as it could raise its funds cheaply at the keenest of interest rates and charge high retail lending rates to consumers, particularly those that bought GE products.

This new activity of GE expanded dramatically but experienced increasing credit losses in the wake of the 2008 financial crash.

You should have stuck to the knitting, guys!

IBM

IBM was the next big guy on my list.

IBM is a technology company with operations in over 170 countries.

IBM produces and sells computer hardware, middleware, and software and provides hosting and consulting services in areas ranging from mainframe computers to nanotechnology.

Shanghai Power, IBM's first pilot venture, had agreed to use IBM's Integrated Distribution Outage Planner.

This foray into China seemed promising.

Surely entering the second largest economy in the world would pay off big time for IBM.

The share price was trading at a relatively low point, despite the possibilities offered by China.

In 2013, I bought 37 shares in IBM at \$178.90, costing €4,975 in total.

What happened to the share price since the purchase?

IBM's stock dropped 19% in 2017, which was particularly noticeable as there was an average gain of 47% in the same year in the S&P 500.

The share price was clearly underperforming the market.

Oops...what's going on!

In 2013, it was widely rumored that the Chinese wanted to direct more power business to domestic firms.

Instead of increased penetration in China, Big Blue delivered the blues!

I sold the shares in July 2017 at \$144.81 a share and made a loss of -€483 after all charges.

It's a pity I couldn't reboot their share price when it crashed on me!

More Large Cap players with a long history in the US of A?

ADT

ADT Corporation began on April 5, 1874, with a night-time security break-in. American District Telegraph (ADT) founder Edward Callahan then created a telegraph-based "callbox" to signal for assistance to a central office.

Today ADT is a leading provider of electronic security, interactive home, and business automation, and monitoring services for residences and small businesses in the United States and Canada.

On 4ᵗʰ June 2014, 200 shares in ADT Corporation were purchased at $32.52 each.

The Euro was worth $1.36, so the US dollar was weak.

When various charges and commissions were added, the purchase amounted to €4,869.

In June 2016, **a further 60 shares were purchased in ADT Corporation at $41.93 each.**

When various charges and commissions were added, the purchase totaled €2,261.

Then, ADT announced that it was to be acquired by private-equity firm Apollo Global Management in a deal valued at about $15 billion.

Under the terms of the deal, ADT shareholders were to receive *$42* in cash for each ADT share they own.

Also...

The US Dollar had strengthened against the Euro. Each Euro was now worth $1.15, down from c.$1.35.

This meant that selling a dollar share and transferring the profits back to Euros enhanced the profit made by almost 20% from the first purchase of ADT shares.

On May 3rd, the acquisition by Apollo was completed, and the sale of the ADT holding generated proceeds of €9,429.

Overall, the Realized Gains from the ADT investments amounted, in Euro terms, to €2,299.

Thank you, thank you, thank you, Mr. Apollo!

Summary of the performance in Selected US Large Cap Companies:

GE	Realized gains	€33
IBM	Realized losses	-€483
ADT	Realized gains	€2,299

In overall terms, the Selected large US companies generated net gains of €1,849.

Although I was lucky with the purchase of ADT by Apollo, I was reaching the conclusion that easy money is difficult to find in the USA.

Let's have a look closer to home and see if I can make money buying UK shares....?

Chapter Fourteen

Buying Close to Home:

Selected UK Large Cap Companies

"What could possibly go wrong?"

WPP plc

In 2019, WPP was considered to be the world's largest advertising company.

It is a British multinational communications, advertising, public relations, and technology company headquartered in London, England.

The share price had recently declined, and hopefully, it was now attractively priced.

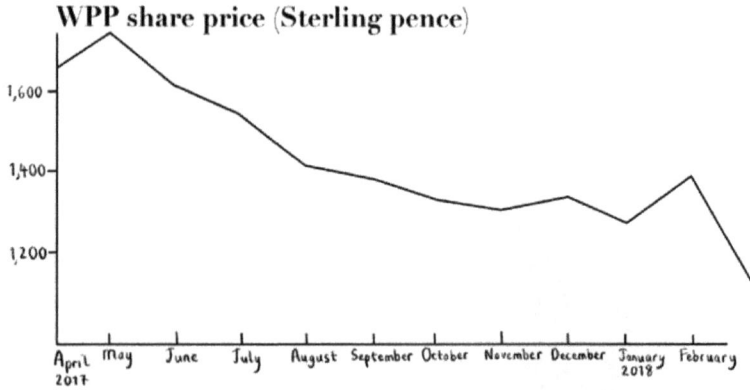

In March 2018, 275 shares in WPP plc were purchased at £10.9141.

The Dividend yield was a satisfactory 4%.

What happened to the share price since the purchase?

The WPP share price declined by 10%, but thankfully an increase in the Sterling/Euro exchange rate partly offset the decline in the share price.

Just before Covid hit, my investment showed an **Unrealized Loss of -€208**.

Hmm.... hardly the best 'advertisement' for investing in the share!

What other UK companies might be worth a flutter?

Carnival plc

Carnival Corporation plc is a British-American cruise operator, currently the world's largest travel leisure company, with a combined fleet of over 100 vessels across 10 cruise line brands. ... Carnival is listed in both the S&P 500 and FTSE 250 indices.

I had been on some cruises, liked them, and expected growing demand for cruise ship services. I felt they would be an increasingly popular holiday option.

In December 2019, I purchased **130 shares in Carnival plc at £31.4678 per share at an all-in cost of €4,925.**

What happened to the share price since the purchase?

The Carnival share price continued to strengthen over the following weeks to £37.08, resulting in **an Unrealized Gain of €738**.

Of course, this was before the official arrival of Covid…more on that later!

Pre-Covid summary of the performance in Selected UK Company shares:

WPP	Unrealized Loss	-208
Carnival	Unrealized Gain	738

Overall, the net Unrealized Gain from the Selected large UK Cap companies amounted to €530.

A very modest result……… nothing to write home about!

I wonder if bricks and mortar investments would have been a better investment.

Chapter Fifteen
Bricks and Mortar Shares:
Property & Construction Companies

"the best investment"

At this point, you, the reader, might understandably be curious whether an alternative investment like property might have been a better prospect than buying shares on the stock market.

Property has a very big advantage as an alternative to shares.

A significant amount of the cost of the property can be borrowed – once you have enough for a deposit!

What is owed to the bank remains fixed, while the proceeds earned from the sale rise as property prices rise.

If the property rises in value, the investor makes a capital gain on all the money that he/she and the bank has invested in the property.

Of course, the investor loses both the money he/she stumped up and the money he/she borrowed if the property falls dramatically in value.

You are betting with other people's money…with the right to pocket the profit earned from the borrowing and from the funds you invested in the property.

It's true that many investors enjoy excellent returns from property, but property can also be a particularly tricky investment.

To invest in property, the initial amount required is usually quite large, often requiring hundreds of thousands of euros.

Property investments also need to be managed and maintained by the investor to ensure that their properties are not 'wrecked' by tenants and that the tenants pay the rent as agreed.

The other big problem is that Property is famously 'illiquid,' meaning if you ever need to access your finance, it can be quite a considerable length of time before sales are completed.

There is another way for an investor to gain exposure to the benefits of property investments without the headache of owning the property:

Investing in property companies rather than the property itself.

REITs (Real Estate Investment Trusts)

REITs are stock market vehicles set up by Governments to promote investment in properties.

These shares are quoted on the stock market and can be readily sold.

Investing in a REIT offers the benefits of property ownership without the headaches or expense of being a landlord.

You don't have to repair the damage to the kitchen yourself!

REITs facilitate investments by individual shareholders in diverse properties such as commercial or residential real estate portfolios, apartment complexes, data centers, healthcare facilities, and hotels.

REITs also invest in infrastructure (e.g., fiber cables, cell towers, and energy pipelines), office buildings, retail centers, and warehouses.

Investing in property through the purchase of shares in REITs delivers the important advantages of liquidity and diversity for a portfolio.

I decided to start local and buy shares in an Irish REIT.

IRES

Irish Residential Properties REIT Plc (**IRES**) purchases and accumulates high quality apartments to rent in the greater Dublin area and is not involved in commercial properties.

The major media outlets in Ireland had reported in 2016 that residential property prices in the Dublin Region had increased by 64.7% from the trough in 2013, with the Society of Chartered Surveyors Ireland anticipating property values to increase by an average of 6.6% in 2017.

The annual rental growth rate to Q3 2016 was 7.1%.

Irish property prices and rents were increasing due to the rising population and inadequate supply of housing:

Population Trends Republic of Ireland (millions)

Much of the increase in population occurred in the greater Dublin area, which was where IRES operated.

Political Risk

Politicians were becoming increasingly concerned about the high cost of accommodation.

New rent increase restrictions were enacted in 2016 that would restrict rents from increasing above 4% per annum.

The issue is that there exists enormous pressure on politicians to increase the housing supply, but good returns (at levels potentially above 4%) will be required to attract private investment finance to fund new projects.

In May 2016, 2,450 IRES shares were purchased at a cost of €2,836.

The share price was €1.1399.

In September 2016, I bought a further 1,395 shares costing €1,646.

The share price at €1.1575 was not materially higher.

In 2019 the Dividend yield was less than expected, and I reckoned I could get a higher Dividend elsewhere.

On the 15th of October 2019, I sold 1,700 IRES shares generating a Realized Gain of €992.

I was reluctant to sell the remainder of the holding as I continued to believe Irish residential property would perform strongly as an investment.

How did the IRES investment perform afterwards?

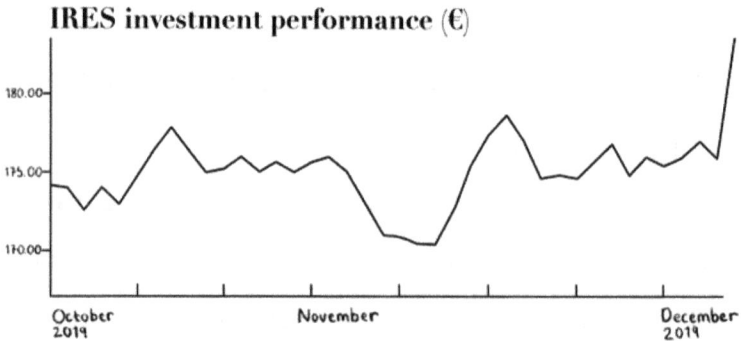

In December 2019, the IRES share price was at a pre-Covid peak of €1.83 with an Unrealized Gain of €1,425.

Overall, the IRES investment had generated, by that time, Realized and Unrealized Gains of €2,417, which was a return of 54% on the original investment of €4,482.

A 54% return in a little over three years compares favorably with equivalent returns from purchasing a physical house or apartment to rent out in the same time frame.

I began searching for similar investments in other European countries.

Germany is the biggest and wealthiest country in the EU.

What about German Property?

The trends in the German stock market (DAX) were moving positively in the latter months of 2016:

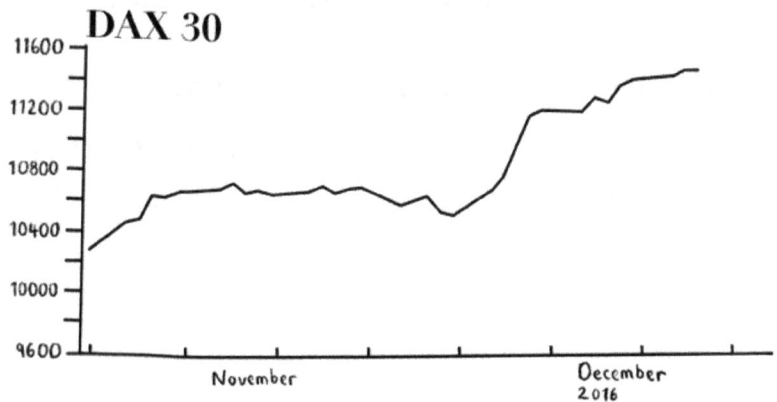

In 2016, Vonovia was Germany's leading nationwide residential real estate company.

Vonovia owned and managed around 355,000 residential units in all of Germany's attractive cities and regions.

ortfolio was valued at approximately €30 billion.

The company was focused on residential property. It was of substantial size and widely quoted on several stock markets, so the shares would be easy to sell if I needed liquidity.

The Dividend yield, at the time, was 3.5%+, and the P/E Ratio was under 10.

It is not often that I can find a share that has both a reasonable Dividend yield and a modest P/E Ratio.

The share was very attractively priced.

In December 2016, I purchased 153 shares in Vonovia at €29.90 each, leading to an all-in cost of €4,627.

How did the Vonovia investment perform?

The share price continued its inexorable rise, but the rise in Dividends did not keep pace with the rise in the share price.

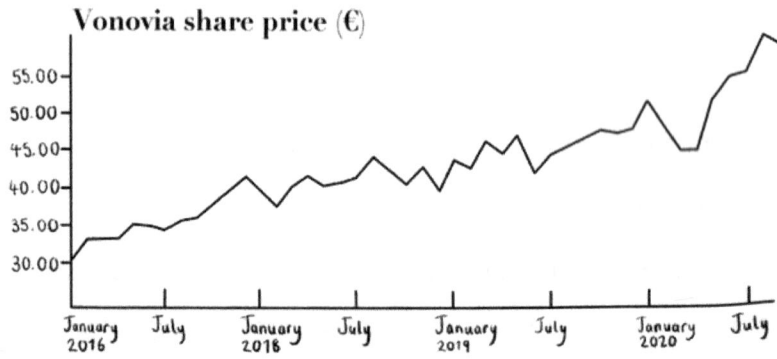

The sale of Vonovia shares

In 2018, the Dividend yield was 3.10%, and I knew I could get higher Dividends elsewhere.

On the 25th of October 2018, I sold 27 Vonovia shares generating Realized Gains of €221.

I held on to the rest of the shares hoping for an upside…but the Dividend yield continued to reduce slightly to 3.09% as the share price continued to climb.

On the 2nd of January 2020, I sold a further 23 Vonovia shares generating more Realized Gains of €359, bringing Total Realized Gains to €580.

How did the share price perform afterward?

The share price rose by 12% in the following six weeks, reaching a pre-Covid peak of €53.28 in February 2020.

By February 21st, I was sitting on Unrealized Gains of €2,412 on the remaining Vonovia shares.

When I added in the Realized Gains from the previous two sales, I had made €2,992 since 2016…a 65% return on the initial investment sum of €4,627.

The return on the Vonovia shareholding compared very favorably with an equivalent return on buying "bricks and mortar."

The IRES and Vonovia investments were in Residential property.

How about the commercial property world in Ireland?

Green REIT

Green REIT had a €1.5bn portfolio that included world-class office, logistics, and retail assets.

Most of these assets were located in and around Dublin.

In the first half of 2017, I bought 3,870 shares in Green REIT, which cost €5,176. The share was trading at a price of €1.39.

What happened to the Green REIT holdings?

Following a strategic review in April 2019, Green REIT put itself up for sale in a bid to "maximize value for its shareholders."

The directors were of the view that the share price undervalued the properties.

If the shareholders sold all the shares to an acquisitive company, they would receive less money than if they sold all the properties directly to purchasers on the open market.

UK Property company Henderson Park bought Green REIT's properties for €1.34 bn giving a fair value for the underlying properties.

The shareholders received €1.91 per share in cash, as a result providing me with a Realized Gain of €1,846 net of transaction costs and the cost of my investment.

When your luck is in...your luck is in!

Where to next?

Unibail Rodamco Westfield is a leading listed European commercial property operator, investor, and developer with a portfolio of high-quality assets valued at €43.1 billion.

The Company operates a portfolio of commercial properties with a focus on shopping centers.

The Company's assets were located primarily in the Netherlands.

The share price was at historic lows, and I hoped it was about to start trending onward and upwards.

In July 2017, I purchased 24 shares at €212.85 each, costing €5,174 in total.

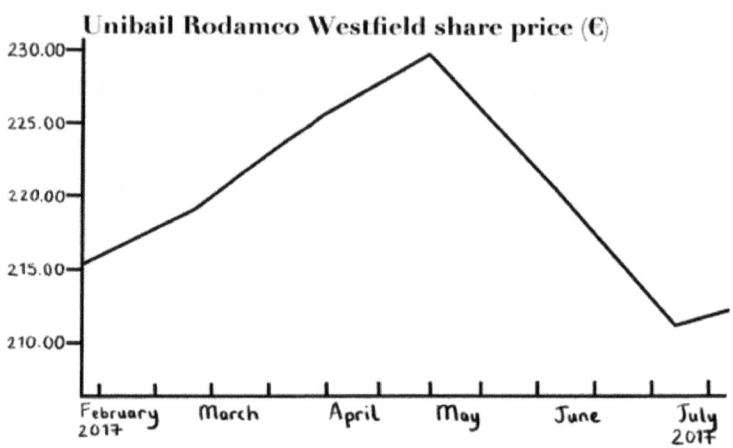

What happened to the share price since then?

The share price had declined by 34% by November 2019.

Crikey...*not a pretty sight!*

What did management do with my money?

In December 2017, Unibail Rodamco acquired the US Westfield Corporation to become the world's premier operator of flagship shopping malls.

Approximately 38.7 million Unibail Rodamco Westfield new shares were issued to Westfield shareholders, and US$5.6 billion was paid as cash consideration.

The issue of new shares immediately reduced the price of existing shares to €127.78 (as the extra shares result in extra shareholders who are entitled to their share of future profits).

187

Unibail Rodamco Westfield was betting that shoppers would continue to be attracted to shopping malls in spite of a growing move to the Internet and home-based shopping.

Will parents continue to bring their kids on a day out to the mall?

Hmm...in the meantime...

This share was nursing an Unrealized Loss, based on its pre-covid peak price, of -€1,769 even though the share price had recovered somewhat to €141.90.

I continued to hold the share because it had an extremely attractive Dividend which was stable even though the share price had fallen.

But was it sustainable?

In 2019, the Financial Analysts covering the company expected an increase in the Dividend, and their consensus forecast advised investors to hold their position in the company.

Basically, hang on unless the Dividend is cut!

I had had enough shopping centers at that point, so I went looking to buy shares in large Construction Companies that had a major presence in their chosen markets.

Barratt Developments

Barratt Developments was the UK's leading housebuilder, and its share price had risen sharply in the previous 12 months.

Maybe it's a winner?

In April 2019, I purchased 820 shares for £6.04 each at an all-in cost of €5,795. The Dividend yield was modest at 3%.

What happened to the Barratt Developments' share price?

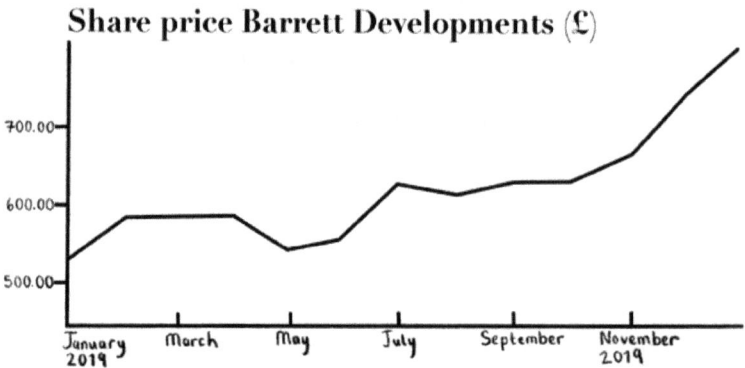

The share price had risen to £8.0 by December 2019., its pre-covid peak price.

I was enjoying Unrealized Gains of €1,983 *Hold on and enjoy!*

I then turned my attention to the major construction companies operating in Ireland.

There was a housing shortage crisis in Ireland which should present opportunities for builders.

Cairn Homes:

Cairn Homes was a prominent Irish homebuilding Company.

They intended to start paying Dividends in 2019.

I bought 3,890 Cairn Homes shares at €1.282 each on 3rd January 2020 for €5,062.

What has happened to the share price since?

The Cairns Homes share price hit a pre-Covid peak some weeks after the purchase generating a modest Unrealized Gain of €151.

Any other Irish Builders? There are a lot more houses needed on the Emerald Isle.

Glenveagh Properties

I purchased 6,690 shares for €0.76 each in Glenveagh Properties on 11th February 2020 at an all-in cost of €5,181.

They don't pay Dividends...*let's give them a go and hope for the best!*

What has happened to the share price since?

The share price hit its pre-Covid peak one week later, at €0.85, generating Unrealized Gains, at that time, of €506.

Still early days!

Pre-Covid Summary of the performance of Property & Construction Companies:

IRES	Unrealized Gain	€1,425
IRES	Realized Gain	€992
Vonovia	Unrealized Gain	€2,412
Vonovia	Realized Gain	€580
Green REIT	Realized Gain	€1,846
Unibail Rodamco Westfield	Unrealized Loss	-€1,769
Barratt Developments	Unrealized Gain	€1,983
Cairn Homes	Unrealized Gain	€151
Glenveagh Properties	Unrealized Gain	€506

Investing in Property & Construction shares generated a very satisfactory overall net return of €8,126 (c.10% per annum).

The investments created generous returns from the property market without dealing with estate agents, property surveys, sourcing tenants, home repairs, etc.

Future Outlook

There continues to be a shortage of housing units in cities across the world as those with existing city properties seek to make it difficult for developers to build large-scale housing units 'in their backyard.'

The pressure on supplying new housing units is exacerbated by growing population numbers.

The pandemic and increasing internet use in work situations have facilitated working from home with more people located in the countryside.

This may result in less froth in commercial and city property prices.

Also, government actions to boost property supply could eventually flood the market with new properties resulting in a lowering of property prices.

The investor needs to remain vigilant if getting involved in property companies. All good stories come to an end!

Finally, for better or worse, I now had built my portfolio.

From 2008 - 2020 I invested almost €200,000 across a wide range of sectors: Banks, Oil & Basic Resources, Automobiles, Pharma, Utilities, UK Retail, Telecoms, Insurance, Irish Small Cap, German Large Cap, US Large Cap, UK Large Cap, Property & Construction. I was primarily chasing Dividend income from Value stocks and maintained a conservative limit of approximately €5,000 per holding.

Now it was time to sit back and enjoy the fruits of my labor...or so I thought!

I had no idea what a Rollercoaster ride was ahead for the portfolio with the arrival of the Covid-19 global pandemic, followed not long afterward by the outbreak of war in Ukraine beginning in February 2022.

How would the portfolio perform in those turbulent times?

Section B

The Roller Coaster Years: 2020 to 2022

Section A followed my journey as I built up a share portfolio starting in 2008 and finishing in early Spring 2020.The Chapters showed the successes and failures experienced as I grappled with the constantly changing circumstances of the stock market.

The ultimate test to establish if my efforts proved worthwhile is best established by the resilience, or otherwise, of the portfolio as market conditions change.

Section B tracks the valuations of the portfolio from early 2020 through to the impact on the shares of the Russian invasion of Ukraine. The Section finishes with a view on the future outlook of the portfolio in the months and years following the invasion.

And if the drama of the rollercoaster years doesn't frighten the reader too much, Section C contains takeaway information on the best strategies when buying and selling shares on the market; how to minimise risk to your money, and a handy 10-step checklist that the reader can use to assess the health of any share when deciding whether to make a purchase.

Chapter Sixteen

Before the Pandemic: February 2020

"Success!"

The effort to build a share portfolio over the twelve-year period from 2008 to 2020 paid off handsomely.

Not all holdings were profitable, but there were more winners than losers, confirming the need to diversify one's holdings and avoid putting 'all your eggs in one basket.'

A quick snapshot of the pre-Covid portfolio in February 2020:

Unrealized Gains – not yet cashed in – all Sectors ahead of cost:

Value of Pre-Covid Portfolio Feb-20 Sector	Original Costs €	Market Values €	Unrealized Gains €	%
Banks	35,530	35,947	417	1%
Oil & Basic Resources	22,051	24,973	2,922	13%
Autos	12,733	17,025	4,292	34%
Pharma	4,603	8,058	3,455	75%
Utilities	19,320	27,025	7,705	40%
UK Retail	4,382	4,402	20	0%
Telecoms	8,123	11,319	3,196	39%
Insurance	50,009	64,549	14,540	29%
Large UK Companies	8,386	8,916	530	6%
Property & Construction	26,827	31,535	4,708	18%
Totals	191,964	233,749	41,785	22%

The biggest success, in Euro terms, was in the **Insurance sector,** accounting for €14,540 of the overall €41,785 in Unrealized Gains, followed by the gains in the **utility sector** of €7,705.

Gains in Utilities were driven by the shares held in **National Grid.**

I invested in 10 different Insurance Companies, primarily in Continental Europe. The holdings **in Aegon and NN Group**, the two Dutch insurers, were the only ones to disappoint.

The **Property & Construction sector** was also performing well at that time.

Vonovia was trading at very satisfactory levels. **Unibail Rodamco Westfield** was well under water as its reliance for future earnings on shopping malls was very badly received by the market.

However, strong gains were recorded by **Barratt Developments**, the UK construction company, and by **IRES,** the Irish REIT.

The Unrealized Gain of €4,292 in the **Auto sector** was mainly down to the very timely (blood in the streets) investment in **Toyota.**

Unrealized Gains in the **Pharma** sector of €3,455 were outstanding, equalling 75% of their cost, due to the US Pharma stocks **Pfizer and AbbVie**.

...two good 'uns, even if I say so myself!

US Telecoms **AT&T and Verizo**n were also performing well at this time.

Small gains occurred in the **Large UK Companies and Retail sectors**.

Banks' shareholdings were slightly ahead of cost, with relatively strong performances in the **Canadian Imperial Bank of Commerce (CIBC)** and the Swiss bank **UBS**.

These Unrealized Gains were largely offset by disappointing performances in the Italian Bank **Intesa San Paolo** and the Scandinavian Bank **Nordea**. The **AIB** shareholding was also trading slightly below cost.

Thank God I didn't have all my funds in Irish bank shares...*once bitten, twice shy!*

The overall Unrealized Gains of €41,785, 22% ahead of costs, reflected very satisfactory valuations in February 2020.

Get over your fear of the stock market...get in and join the party!

Now let's look at Realized Gains – where shares were sold with an eye on profit...*cash is king!*

Pre-Covid 2008 - 2020	Realized Gains €
Banks	8,264
Oil & Basic Resources	4,533
Autos	-2,408
Pharma	1,227
Utilities	-3,924
UK Retail	-1,172
Telecoms	-2,603
Insurance	1,053
Irish Small Cap Companies	17,541
Large Cap UK Companies	0
Large Cap German Companies	4,953
Large Cap US Companies	1,849
Property & Construction	3,418
Totals	32,731

The **small local (Irish) companies** delivered the goodies big time!

The Realized Gain**s in the Banking Sector** were also very pleasant.

Fortune favors the brave!

The investments in the German companies **Siemens and SAP** were very satisfactory, while the sale of **Tullow Oil**

Nowadays with more experience under my belt in chasing dividends I expect much bigger dividends than when I started building the portfolio. **But I do need to know if my 3.5% modest target was achieved?**

Dividends Sector	Portfolio Market Values February 2020 €	Dividends €	Portfolio Original Costs February 2020 €	Gross Dividend Yield on costs %
Banks	35,947	1,982	35,530	5.58%
Oil & Basic Resources	24,973	1,546	22,051	7.01%
Autos	17,025	544	12,733	4.27%
Pharma	8,058	363	4,603	7.89%
Utilities	27,025	1,278	19,320	6.62%
UK Retail	4,402	239	4,382	5.45%
Telecom	11,319	539	8,123	6.64%
Insurance	64,549	3,226	50,009	6.45%
Large UK Companies	8,916	484	8,386	5.77%
Property & Construction	31,535	823	26,827	3.07%
Totals	233,749	11,024	191,964	5.74%

The **Gross Dividend Yield of 5.74%** comfortably exceeded my 3.5% target.

By 2020, the Dividends that my shares had generated gave me a gross annual income of **€11,024,** enabling me to enhance my lifestyle!

This was much better than putting my moolah on deposit in the bank!

Was I pleased with the performance of my portfolio?

Buoyant Unrealized Gains, significant Realized Gains, and noticeable annual cash in from Dividends.

But of course!

> *I see trees of green, red roses too.*
> *I see them bloom for you and me.*
> *And I think to myself,*
> *What a wonderful world!*
> *(Louis Armstrong)*

But wait   *But wait*
     But wait   *But wait*
       But wait   *But wait*
     But wait

Oh no…... V stands for Virus………...

Chapter Seventeen
The Arrival of The Novel Coronavirus
Covid-19

"Looks like my shares
caught Covid..."

A New Market Shock:

Bye, bye Miss American Pie

Put my savings in the markets,

But the markets made me cry.

Don McLean...(misquoted)

On March 11, 2020, the World Health Organisation (WHO) declared the novel coronavirus (Covid-19) outbreak to be a global pandemic.

Financial markets plunged with dizzying speed.

The US, German, and London stock prices peaked on Valentine's Day 2020, and by March 23rd, 2020, they were each 35% lower.

This week of March 23rd, 2020, was the worst week for stocks since the 2008/9 financial crisis.

Portfolios collapsed as business revenues were lost and supply chains were frozen.

It did not matter which stock market you were invested in.

The effect was global.

What happened to my portfolio?

My portfolio declined by 43% from its pre-Covid valuation.

Impact of the Covid Pandemic				
Sector	February 2020 €	March 2020 €	February to March Decline €	%
Banks	35,947	17,691	-18,256	-51%
Oil & Basic Resources	24,973	13,096	-11,877	-48%
Autos	17,025	11,871	-5,154	-30%
Pharma	8,058	5,883	-2,175	-27%
Utilities	27,025	19,735	-7,290	-27%
UK Retail sector	4,402	3,156	-1,246	-28%
Telecoms	11,319	8,780	-2,539	-22%
Insurance	64,549	34,381	-30,169	-47%
Large UK Companies	8,916	2,420	-6,496	-73%
Property & Construction	31,535	16,460	-15,075	-48%
Totals	233,749	133,473	-100,276	-43%

The destruction in valuations was just over **€100,000,** and it occurred suddenly and without warning in a relatively short period of time.

Not a pretty sight, I have to say...!

How did each sector in my portfolio cope?

Large Cap UK Companies experienced a **73% fall** in valuations:

The Impact of the Covid Pandemic on My Large Cap UK Shares				
February 2020 – March 2020				
Company	February 2020	March 2020	Decline from February 2020 - March 2020	
	€	€	€	%
WPP	3,253	1,516	-1,737	-53%
Carnival Cruises	5,663	904	-4,759	-84%
Totals	8,916	2,420	-6,496	-73%

WPP was a large advertising agency.

Good luck with that in a pandemic!

As for **Carnival Cruises Lines:**

Carnival Cruise Lines was the owner of the ill-fated Diamond Princess - one of many ships that found themselves bounced from port to port in March 2020 – not allowed to dock and disembark its passengers due to the presence of the virus onboard.

Travel bans were being enforced across the world, and the US Centre For Disease Control and Prevention (CDC) had released a 'no-sail' order for cruise ships.

So, global operators canceled scheduled trips for the foreseeable future.

This cruise company was clearly up *that* creek without a paddle!

The **Banking Sector** also **declined by 51%.** Was the disruption to the economy going to result in big increases in Bad Debts?

Such an event would not be good for Banks........... investors exited Bank shares, particularly in the smaller countries of The Netherlands and Ireland.

The Impact of the Covid Pandemic on My Banking Shares				
February 2020 – March 2020				
Company	February 2020	March 2020	Decline from February 2020 to March 2020	
	€	€	€	%
ING	5,612	1,978	-3,634	-65%
CIBC	6,109	3,467	-2,642	-43%
Intesa Sanpaolo	4,124	2,457	-1,667	-40%
Nordea Bank	4,564	2,665	-1,899	-42%
UBS	6,115	3,528	-2,587	-42%
Banco Santander	5,139	2,626	-2,513	-49%
AIB	4,284	970	-3,314	-77%
Totals	35,947	17,691	-18,256	-51%

Oil & Basic Resources

Oil & Basic Resources (in addition to Bank stocks) are highly Cyclical stocks that would be expected to perform poorly in these 'bad times' as the pandemic took hold.

When economies slow down, then demand slows dramatically for commodities such as Oil and Basic Resources.

Investors quickly sold out and drove these share prices down and down.

The horror of horrors!

The Impact of the Pandemic on My Oil & Basic Resources Shares February 2020 – March 2020				
Company	February 2020 €	March 2020 €	Decline from Februar to March y 2020 2020 €	%
Total Energies	4,920	2,603	-2,317	-47%
Rio Tinto	5,568	2,708	-2,860	-51%
BHP	7,172	3,486	-3,686	-51%
BASF	3,772	2,158	-1,614	-43%
Covestro	3,541	2,141	-1,400	-40%
Totals	24,973	13,096	-11,877	-48%

The **Oil & Basic Resources Sector** fell by more than the average 43% fall in the overall Portfolio:

Basic Resources stocks fared very badly, and **BHP** and **Rio Tinto** fared the most badly in the overall Sector.

As the pandemic progressed, demand for their products was sharply reduced as their customers' factories were locked down in many countries.

The **Property & Construction** sector was also very much a laggard:

People buy new homes in good times, but when times are tough, most large "spends," such as home purchases, are postponed until families are sure they have successfully navigated through to the good times.

The outlook for properties and construction companies was dire....to say the least.

Batten down the hatches and hold on to your savings!

The Impact of the Covid Pandemic on Property & Construction Shares				
February 2020 – March 2020				
Company	February 2020	March 2020	Decline from February 2020 to March 2020	
	€	€	€	%
IRES	3,925	2,124	-1,802	-46%
Vonovia	5,527	4,349	-1,178	-21%
Unibail Rodamco Westfield	3,406	1,207	-2,199	-65%
Barratt Developments	7,778	3,225	-4,553	-59%
Cairn Homes	5,213	2,412	-2,801	-54%
Glenveagh Properties	5,687	3,144	-2,542	-45%
Totals	31,535	16,460	-15,075	-48%

Unibail Rodamco Westfield was anticipated to be very adversely affected as many of their shopping tenants remained shut during the pandemic.

Shops could no longer pay the rent, as very few customers ventured outdoors.

Vonovia, the owner of a wide selection of mature German residential properties, experienced a relatively modest fall of 21%

IRES, the Irish REIT, disappointed as people harked back to the previous Irish property crash.

Cairn Homes and Barratt Developments were finding it difficult to complete construction work and make sales during government imposed "lockdowns".

The builder, Glenveagh Properties had bought back their own shares keeping their share price relatively high. Surely not a vote in the future!

Insurance *Could Insurance Companies be sued under Business Continuity policies?*

The Impact of the Covid Pandemic on My Insurance Shares February 2020 – March 2020				
Company	February 2020 €	March 2020 €	Decline from February to March 2020 2020 €	%
Aviva	5,895	2,898	-2,997	-51%
Munich Re	5,060	2,769	-2,290	-45%
Zurich	11,076	7,559	-3,517	-32%
Axa	5,650	2,810	-2,840	-50%
Allianz	9,744	4,998	-4,746	-49%
Swiss Re	6,911	3,357	-3,555	-51%
Generali	6,486	3,637	-2,849	-44%
Aegon	2,035	835	-1,200	-59%
NN Group	4,878	2,813	-2,065	-42%
Legal & General	6,815	2,705	-4,110	-60%
Totals	64,549	34,381	-30,169	-47%

Aegon Life Insurance was heavily involved in the US, and the adverse share price movement reflected a lack of confidence in the company's business model there, allied to the post-Covid hit to valuations.

The weakness in sterling accounted for 8%+ of the post-Covid adverse swing in the **Legal & General Insurance and Aviva** holdings.

The share price of the Swiss reinsurance company, **Swiss Re,** disappointed as market participants were cautious given the relatively high level of risks taken by this Re-insurer.

The share price of **Munich Re**, the other Reinsurance Company in the portfolio, performed satisfactorily.

The market clearly had its favorites.

Zurich Insurance, Generali, and NN Group suffered less than others.

Shares in the **highly Cyclical Auto Sector** performed surprisingly well as they declined by 30%, well below the 43% decline in the overall Portfolio.

The Impact of the Covid-19 Pandemic on My Autos Shares:

February 2020 – March 2020				
Company	Feb 2020	Mar 2020	Decline from February 2020 to March 2020	
	€	€	€	%
Toyota	6,133	4,813	-1,320	-22%
VW	5,992	2,965	-3,027	-51%
Bridgestone	4,900	4,094	-806	-16%
Totals	17,025	11,871	-5,154	-30%

VW fell in line with expectations for Cyclical shares, but the performance of the Japanese shares surprised on the upside.

Why did the Japanese buck the trend suffered by VW?

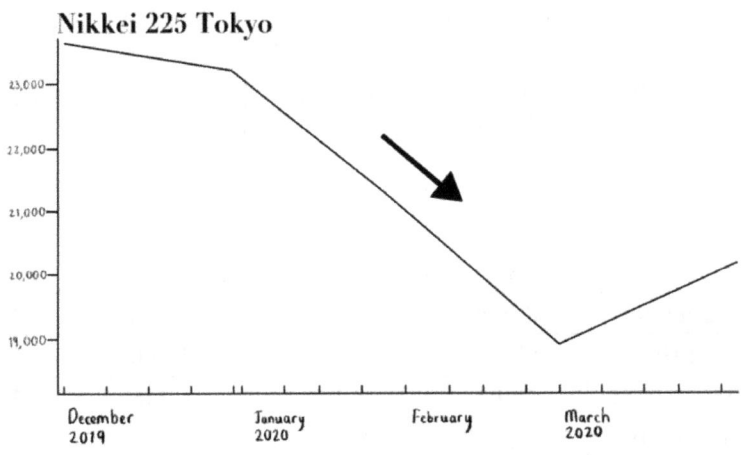

Nikkei 225 Tokyo

The Japanese shares did not experience such a dramatic drop because the Japanese market had already been experiencing declines in December 2019 and January 2020, when Western markets were still moving upwards.

The sudden decline in Western markets in February and March was more severe as they caught up with the earlier trend experienced by Japanese shares. The fact that the Japanese markets declined earlier presumably means the seriousness of the Covid-19 virus was recognized earlier in Japan, as the virus had originated in China/Asia.

Defensive Sectors: If my Defensive shares were truly Defensive, then I would have anticipated smaller declines than the average. The Defensive Sectors declines were well below the Portfolio average decline of 43%, (as expected):

Defensive Sector	Pre-Covid Market Values at Peak	Post-Covid Market Values	Decline in Market Values Pre-to Post Covid	% Decline in Market Values
	€	€	€	%
Pharma	8,058	5,883	-2,175	-27%
Utilities	27,025	19,735	-7,290	-27%
UK Retail	4,402	3,156	-1,246	-28%
Telecoms	11,319	8,780	-2,539	-22%
Totals	50,804	37,554	-13,250	-26%

Good on you guys.... keep up the good work!

So, how did I react to all this bad news?

My heart followed my ass right down into my boots!

The only saving grace was that the Dividends continued to be paid and this cash provided sufficient liquidity to ensure that forced sales were not required at this very worst time.

Has the time come to sit tight, lock away my investments, and do nothing till the pandemic is tamed?

Where was I at this stage in my stock market journey?

This book began with the Stock Market Crash of 2008-09, which resulted from a crisis in the financial system in the United States after a period of excessive speculation in the US housing market

We saw the S&P 500 decline by more than 50 percent in 2008/9.

The crash spread to other countries: Canada, Mexico, and countries in Europe and the rest of the world that have close trading relations with the United States and Europe.

But the markets recovered!

Then along came the Pandemic, in Spring 2020.

This Pandemic had originated in China and spread to Europe before making its way to North America.

Now we had another stock market crash because of the spread of the Covid-19 Pandemic.

Although the crash was less severe than that experienced during the previous crash, the speed of the decline was much quicker.

Was the arrival of Covid an opportunity to buy?

There certainly was much more 'Blood on the streets'...

Chapter Eighteen

Blood in the Streets:

An Opportunity to Buy Cyclicals

"It's time to get on board"

The recovery began so quickly that it might have been a "dead cat bounce," a phrase that is used to describe a period when share prices experienced a brief resurgence followed by a severe decline.

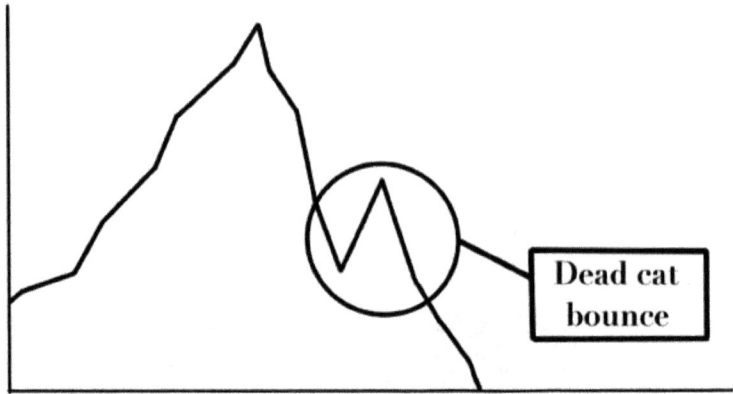

The risk facing investors following the stock market crash in March 2020 was that they would buy shares before they truly bottomed.

I was wary of falling for a 'dead cat bounce,' so I watched the Charts closely in each market until I could see a sustained uplift.

By April 2020, the S&P 500 had moved above its post-Covid crash level:

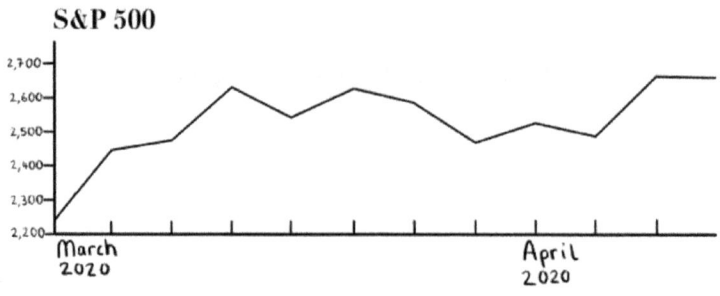

The FTSE 100 was also trending upwards:

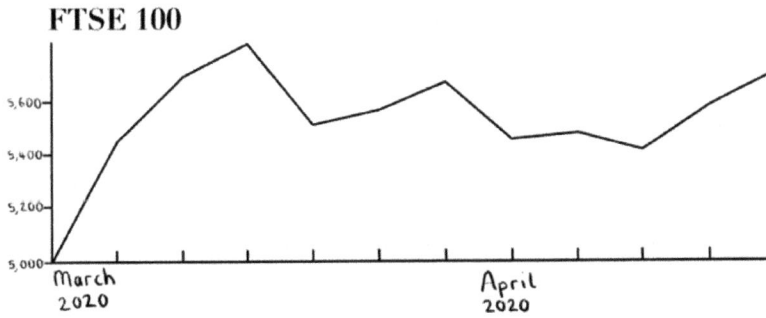

The German DAX did not disappoint; it also experienced an upward trajectory:

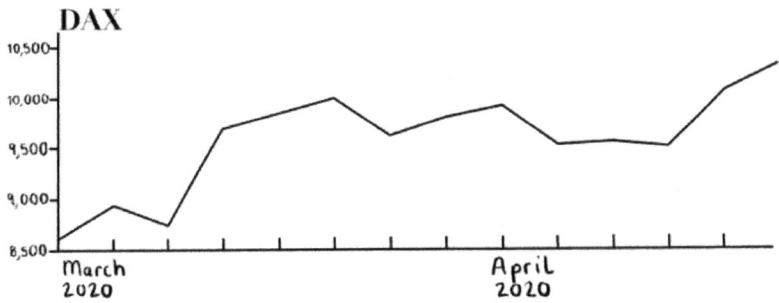

By early April, the major markets were rising in tandem.

Could I be optimistic, or were these movements a dead cat bounce?

In the US: The Fed was providing cheap loans to the US Government to enable it to support the Government through the pandemic induced economic crisis.

On March 15, 2020, the US Federal Reserve/Central Bank said that it would buy at least $500 billion in US Government Bonds and $200 billion in government-guaranteed mortgage-backed securities over "the coming months."

This enabled the US Government to afford support programs to help Businesses and Households to deal with the Crash.

In the UK: The Bank of England supported the UK Government by providing them with finance at negligible interest rates.

The UK Government, then, was also able to fund massive support programs for Households and Businesses.

In the EU: The ECB began to buy up commercial debt in the financial markets, thereby ensuring new debt could be issued very cheaply by Banks, Businesses, and Governments.

Banks were also offered long term loans at a negative interest rate.

The ECB accepted a much broader set of assets as collateral, including loans of small size to small and medium-sized enterprises (SMEs) or even self-employed workers, and these assets were accepted at more favorable conditions.

All Governments were then able to borrow and support their economies at virtually negligible interest rates.

Against this backdrop of concerted action by the world's fiscal and monetary authorities, I took the view that the improvement in share prices was here to stay.

I re-entered the Markets on 6th April, three weeks after the markets had crashed.

Wish me luck!

What causes a stock market recovery?

A sharp contraction in economic activity causes stock markets to suffer a very severe decline as the economic actors – Households and Businesses – stop spending.

Businesses will be expected to sell less, and their earnings fall. Investors immediately mark down stock prices, trying to position themselves for where the economy will be in six months' time.

However, if we use a housing analogy: as house prices fall, people eventually are tempted back into the market. They begin to buy houses, and house prices start to rise.

Low priced stocks eventually tempt investors to start buying again.

The trick is to buy near the bottom and watch your stocks move upward as economic activity recovers.

We saw from the previous market crash that buying Cyclical stocks proved a shrewd strategy.

Will it work again now?

Oil & Basic Resources

As the economy returns to health, demand should return for the Basic Resources required by Manufacturing Industry.

It was to be expected that the share price of these Cyclical stocks would greatly increase.

Rio Tinto

A Cyclical Basic Resources/Mining stock like Rio Tinto is a classic purchase when markets are down.

Before the arrival of Covid-19, this share was trading at a pre-Covid 'high' of €59.35. The pandemic meant the share price was now in the bargain bin.

So, on 6 April 2020, I bought 42 shares at €37.965 for a total cost of €1,850.

Then, on 20 May 2020, I added 86 more shares at €42.83 for a total cost of €4,193.

The Dividend yield was 5.25% in February 2020 but had risen to 6.5%+ in April 2020, which was a major attraction.

The yield was so high because the share price had fallen so low.

Covestro

Another Cyclical share…

The original holding in Covestro had been bought just at the pre-Covid 19 peak in February 2020 when the shares were trading at €38.95.

The Covestro holding had been carrying Unrealized Losses post the Covid crash of -€1,252, and these were of concern.

I decided to add an additional 57 shares to my existing holding in Covestro, the German Plastics company, at a price of €29.37 and an all-in cost of €1,715, bringing the overall stake in the company up to €5,000.

It was hoped that purchasing extra shares at the low price of €29.37 would facilitate exit at breakeven once a recovery occurred in the share price, which it did.

Purchasing the extra 57 shares at €29.37 v the original 86 shares purchased at €38.95 is called averaging down (to an average price excluding charges of €35.13).

It means I can sell out of Covestro at €35.13 (+ charges) and breakeven on the shareholding.

On 15 July 2020, I sold virtually the entire holding in Covestro (140 shares) at a price of €36.90, which generated a small cash profit of €111, a breakeven exit.

The point of the exercise was achieved……….. breakeven plus.

But was the exit well-timed?

.... Hmm!

The share price dipped as July unfolded but then took off on the run.

I could have sold in October at €45 a share.

No point in crying over spilled milk...it wasn't to be!

So...no regrets; a small profit had been made.

Meanwhile, I continued to invest in the Cyclical Oil & Basic Resources sector:

BHP Group

I purchased an additional 125 shares at £16.6858 per share in the mining company, the BHP Group, at an all-in cost of €2,353.

The Dividend yield of 6.75% was very attractive.

By the end of the year, the share had risen by 8%, a similar % to that experienced by Rio Tinto, my other mining Stock.

TotalEnergies

Total Oil had decided to change its name to TotalEnergies.

Let's hope they can walk the talk!

The Dividend yield was 8.27%...*hopefully, most of that will last!*

On 19th August 2020, I bought 144 shares in TotalEnergies at €32.9 per share.

By December 2020, the share price had risen by a similar % to that experienced by the mining Basic Resources shares.

The economy should strengthen as Covid is tamed, and Cyclical share prices should continue to rise.

Let's have a look at Banks – another Cyclical share.

I had made big profits following the financial crash of 2008/9 through investment in bank shares.

Shares in banks with the highest capital ratios (capital held against money loaned out) are well positioned to recover as markets recover.

Irish lenders hold 2.4 times more costly capital against their main lending product, mortgages, than the EU average. That makes them a safer bet.

AIB

AIB's capital ratio was 16.5%+ compared to 13.5% for the Bank of Ireland. AIB was definitely a safer bet.

The share was trading at c. 0.25 times book value (P/B Ratio) which appeared to be overly conservative and suggested that a considerable upside in the share price was likely as the effects of the pandemic receded.

With such a low P/B ratio, the market seemed to be betting that AIB would lose three-quarters of its book value in 2020.

I doubted that, as the central bank had a very tight rein on banking activities in Ireland.

I reckoned that the share price was trading at a bargain.

Purchases:

Dates	Quantities	Price	Cost
29/04/2020	3700	€1.22	€4,589
11/05/2020	1000	€0.96	€983

The first purchase proved to be relatively expensive, while the (smaller) latter purchase was better timed.

These AIB investments would test panic buttons in the next few years though I remained committed to them.

Banco Santander

On 11th December 2029, Banco Santander paid a "scrip Dividend" to my Portfolio.

Instead of receiving the Dividend in cash, 57 additional Santander shares were issued worth the value of the Dividend (€130).

Scrip Dividends are exempt from stamp duty and dealing charges which makes them worthwhile for the investor, and the Bank holds on to the cash it would have paid out in a cash Dividend, so they are attractive to Banks and Investors.

Surely a sensible move in uncertain Covid times!

Nordea Bank

I was worried that Scandinavian Banks were being accused of facilitating money laundering, so I took the decision to exit.

On 21st December 2020, I sold all the shares in Nordea Bank.

I realized a loss on sale of -€1,791.

When you are afraid of a share, get out as fast as you can!

I had enough new Cyclicals and, just as I did in the aftermath of the Financial Crash, I thought I should also chase some Defensives.

Chapter Nineteen
Buying Caution in the Wind:
An Opportunity to Buy Defensives

"Aha! Let me make a quick
phone call"

It is important when investing during a crisis not to put all your eggs in the 'Cyclicals' basket.

As we know, Defensive companies operate businesses where demand for their products and services remains strong in recessionary times.

They do not need to drop their prices to entice their customers back.

The customers never go away.

I started to look for Defensive stocks where the Dividend yield was attractive due to the somewhat depressed price of the company's share price.

Utilities – for starters

Enbridge

I added more shares to my existing holding in Enbridge, the Canadian energy pipeline company.

Purchases:

Date	Quantity	Price	Cost
07/04/2020	60	CAD $41	€1,667
07/07/2020	128	CAD $40.96	€3,472
07/07/2020	20	CAD $40.93	€578

The Dividend yield of 7%+ and the continued diversified exposure to Canada were major attractions.

What happened then?

The Enbridge share price declined by almost 10% to CAD $38...*ouch!*

Yet I noticed that several Financial Analysts who were following the stock were predicting the share price to rise to CAD $51.00.

The analysts also expected Dividends to increase by 9.96%.

I will hold on for the moment and pocket the Dividends.

Let's hope the experts are right!

EDP Portuguese Energy Company

On 18/08/2020, I took up a rights issue and bought 114 shares at €3.30 a share, costing €376 in total.

The Dividend yield was 5.5%.

A small bargain purchase.... never look a gift horse in the mouth!

Edison International

This group is a major player in Southern California, where it provides 13 million people with electricity.

Since 1980 Edison International were focusing more on renewable energy. At least 46% of the fuel Edison uses to generate power comes from clean energy (6% nuclear power, the rest from other renewable energy sources, including biomass and wind).

The Edison International share price had continued to rise steadily, and the Dividend yield of 4.2% was ok.

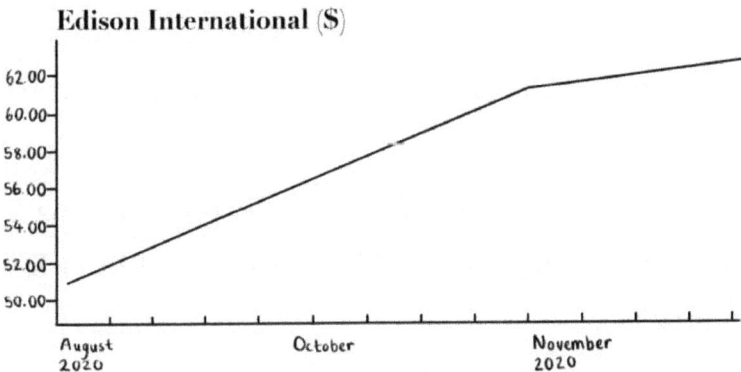

Edison International ($)

On October 21st, 2020, 22 Edison International shares were purchased for €3,649.

Any other Defensives?

How about Consumer Staples...maybe UK Retail?

Consumer staples have strong Defensive characteristics.

Mankind must have groceries!

Sainsbury's

I bought an additional 440 Sainsbury's shares at £2.09 per share on 6th April 2020 at an all-in cost of €1,073.

This price was 10% below the price paid on the existing holding.

The Dividend yield was 5.5%.

Then a few weeks later…*horror of horrors!*

Sainsbury's cut their Dividend!

A cut in Dividends signals that the Company expects a 'lousy' future…

Given the lack of a Dividend, I exited the share and took the pain.

On the 20th of May 2020, I sold the entire holding in Sainsbury's at a price of £1.829 per share, realizing a loss of -€1,298.

Defensive? You must be joking!

Pharma stocks are definitely Defensive shares.

Let's give them a go…

Bayer Pharmaceuticals

Bayer is a German company in Healthcare/ Pharmaceuticals and Biotechnology.

In June 2020, Bayer agreed to cough up nearly $11 billion to resolve thousands of US lawsuits claiming that its widely sold Roundup weedkiller caused cancer.

The settled cases represented about 95% of the cases set for trial.

And, as part of the deal, Bayer would pay up to $9.6 billion to settle all the existing cases, including the 30,000 that had not yet been settled.

The overall sum also put aside $1.25 billion for resolving any future claims.

Surely the weedkiller bad news was, at this stage, long built into the share price.

From here on in….it must be onwards and upwards.

On 15/07/2020, I bought 80 Bayer shares at €64.25 each for €5,194 total.

The Dividend yield was almost 5%.

The share price steadily declined, so I bought a further 125 shares at the "knockdown "price of €46.285 for each share, costing €5,843.

I got the 125 shares for almost the same cost as the 80 shares.

My ass was truly out the window now!

The share price was relatively stable through the Summer of 2020, so maybe things will work out.

Let's see if I am right…!

Viatris

In November 2020, Pfizer Inc decided to float off some of its products into a newly listed company called Viatris. Lipitor and Viagra were among the products involved.

My portfolio was allocated sixteen free shares with an opening value of €126. This was not a 'world shattering' event for me. Let us see what the future brings for my tiny holding in Viatris!

AT&T

Telecoms is a Defensive sector: Nobody can live without their phone.

AT&T share price ($)

However, the trend in the AT&T share price was truly awful.

Time to get out!

Even the generous Dividend yield of 7%+ was not attracting buyers into the stock…*surely a danger sign!*

I sold my holding and realized a loss of -€514…*very little harm done!*

Property

In Dublin, demand for places to live continued to be much higher than the availability of homes.

IRES - people must live somewhere.

On 6 April 2020, I bought additional shares in IRES, the Irish residential property REIT, more than tripling the holding:

Dates	Quantities	Prices	Costs
06/04/2020	2100	€1.15	2,463
15/05/2020	1455	€1.18	1,746
22/05/2020	978	€1.19	1,194
27/05/2020	840	€1.27	1,089

The Dividend yield of 4.5% was OKish, and the properties were of high quality, mainly in the better off areas of Dublin City.

The share price had fallen from its pre-Covid peak by almost 40%.

People need to live somewhere, and that need will ensure that the IRES share price is likely to recover.

Vonovia

Vonovia is a residential landlord mainly operating in Germany.

Vonovia's Dividend yield of less than 3% was unattractive and encouraged an exit.

The shareholding had generated high Unrealized Gains due to sharp increases in the share price since the original purchase:

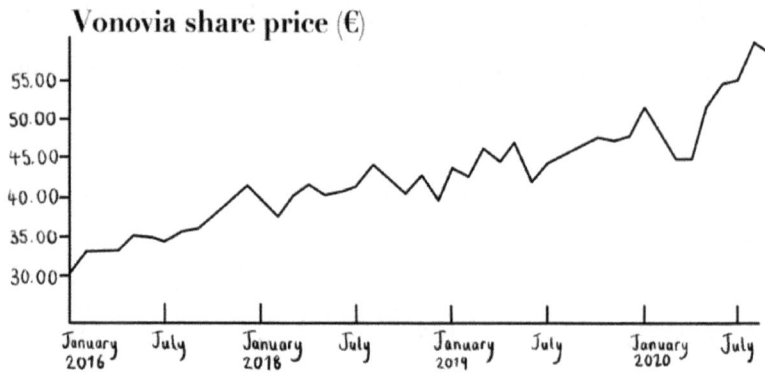

It was time to quit while I was ahead!

In September 2020, I decided to exit the share.

As it turned out, the total Realized Gains of €2,806 from this sale were higher than the Unrealized Gains value of €2,373 <u>before</u> the Covid-19 crash....*very satisfying indeed!*

With these additional Cyclical and Defensive purchases made, I turned my attention to the rest of the portfolio.

How had the Covid-19 pandemic affected the other companies whose shares I held?

Were there shares elsewhere in my portfolio that were languishing with poor outlooks?

I knew I should consider switching out of shares with an uncertain future due to the pandemic - and try my luck elsewhere.

We would lose money on the switches, but would the new shareholdings make up for these losses?

Chapter Twenty

Take Some Pain:

Switch into Stocks with a Better Future

"Let's make room for new growth"

I was looking at some shares in which I had lost confidence.

It was time to do a bit of, as the gardeners say, "deadheading."

...in fact, I knew I needed to dig them shares out, roots and all, and buy some new ones!

Let's start with Unibail Rodamco Westfield.

Aside from the pandemic, shopping malls cannot do well as shoppers move online.

I sold the entire holding in Unibail Rodamco Westfield.

Shares that had been bought in July 2017 for €212.85 per share were sold in May 2020 at €42.64, realizing losses of -€4,192.

A hefty loss in any language.

This loss was a little higher than the -€3,968 loss prevailing at the time of the post-Covid crash, proving there is no excuse for sitting on one's hands and hoping for the best.

Take your punishment on the chin.

However painful though this Realized Loss was, things got much worse as the summer progressed.

The Unibail Rodamco Westfield share went down to €35.......

it was a narrow escape.

Barratt Developments

Was my investment in the UK's largest housebuilder a safe one?

I had currency concerns relating to Brexit, and the Barratt Board had also decided not to pay a Dividend!

On 19 August 2020, I sold the entire holding in the UK Builder **Barratt Developments**.

This sale realized losses of -€1,093, which compared favorably with the Unrealized Losses of -€2,570 prevailing when Covid arrived.

Large Cap UK Companies

WPP

At first, I was tempted to add to my holding in WPP, a multinational devoted to advertising and media.

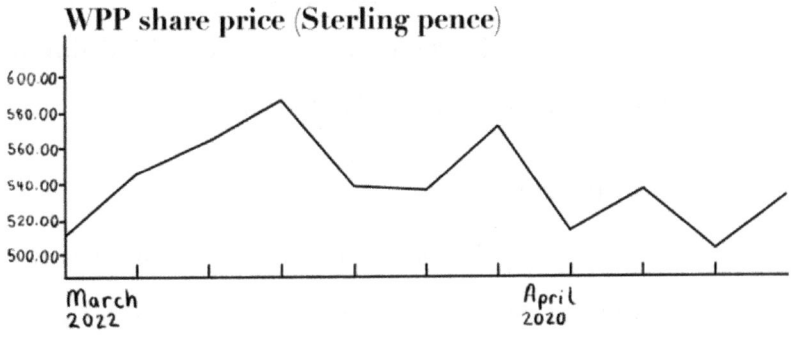

This share price had been stable and had shown very little recovery from its post-Covid low.

Maybe an upside was waiting to happen…?

The WPP share price was trading, at this time, at half the price I paid for the shares bought in 2018.

An opportunity to reduce the very significant losses facing that first purchase, by averaging down the overall cost of the WPP holding, was very attractive.

On 6 April 2020, I purchased 268 shares at £5.084 each for €1,578.

Oh, please, please, don't let me down.

I promise I won't skip your ads ever again!

And so, what happened…the shares rose…*Hallelujah!*

However, I was afraid to stay in WPP due to continuing concerns about the fallout from Brexit, on top of the global pandemic.

I sold the entire WPP holding on 19ᵗʰ May 2020 at a price of £5.93 per share, realizing net losses of -€1,482, a bit better than the Unrealized Loss of -€1,714 sitting in the portfolio when Covid first arrived.

Carnival Cruise Line

I was also worried about Carnival Cruise Line shares.

Who in their right mind was going on a cruise this year?

In June 2020, I sold the entire holding of Carnival at £13.27 a share, ratcheting up a substantial loss of -€2,999.

Lonely are the brave!

This hurt me more than I care to remember!

Later, the share price fell as low as £9 by November 2020.

Phew!

The Realized Losses incurred were c. €1,000 lower than the immediate post-Covid crash Unrealized Losses of -€3,947.94.

A disaster snatched from the jaws of an even nastier defeat!

These Large Cap UK companies...fare thee well!

Now that the vulnerable shares had been sold, I had money to invest somewhere else.

Any new Value shares with generous Dividends?

Chapter Twenty One

Buying Value: Pocketing the Dividends

"Let's bury some dividends"

The decision to exit shares with a poor outlook had freed up some capital that I now needed to invest in other companies.

Given the uncertain outlook in the first year of the pandemic, I felt it was safest to focus on Value Shares with good Dividends that would preserve my income and protect my capital.

My earlier experiences with Insurance had seen me come to adore Insurance shares.

If you like a share and can buy more...well, what are you waiting for!

Munich Re

The Munich Re holding was increased with the following purchases:

Dates	Quantities	Prices	Costs
07/04/2020	8	€189.75	€1,559
19/05/2020	19	€189.65	€3,629

These purchase prices paid were much higher than the €135.35 paid for the 2013 purchase, but the Dividend yield of 5.25% was very attractive.

The Munich Re shareholding's Unrealized Losses, due to the arrival of Covid-19, had been modest at -€290.49, leading me to believe the share price was resilient and would rise in the future.

Boy, that proved to be so true…

By the end of December 2020, overall Unrealized Gains were north of 14%.

You little beauty you!

Munich Re's share should benefit further because it can be argued that the reinsurers have sufficient pricing power to increase premia next year to recover any unexpectedly large Covid-19-related losses this year.

The Dividends are likely to be sustained for the same reason.

Aegon

I also added 1,110 shares to the existing shareholding in Aegon, the Dutch Insurance company, on the 7th of April 2020

The price was €2.45 per share, and the purchase cost all in was €2,767, bringing my total investment in Aegon to €5,000+.

The share was off its post-Covid low and was trading in a stable range.

The upside might occur when the economy recovers.

What happened then?

Unfortunately, the trend in the Aegon share price went into reverse.

I became afraid that there were those 'in the know' who were escaping from the share.

What did they know that I didn't?

On the 21st of May 2020, I sold almost my entire holding (1,607 shares) at €2.203 per share, realizing losses of -€1,938,

I had slightly increased the Unrealized Losses estimated at -€1,842 at the time that Covid-19 struck.

And then Reuters provided critical information:

Aegon reported lower-than-expected first-half earnings on Thursday as the coronavirus pandemic led to higher mortality and lower interest rates in the United States, where it does two-thirds of its business.

Aegon will now cut its interim Dividend to **6 cents from 15 cents**.

The company would use any cash for the time being to reduce leverage and strengthen the balance sheet.

The company reported that solvency had declined to 195% from 201% at the end of 2019.

And yet, subsequently, the sale undertaken by me on May 21st turned out to be the massacre of the innocents.

…look what happened to the share price after the sale…it went up!

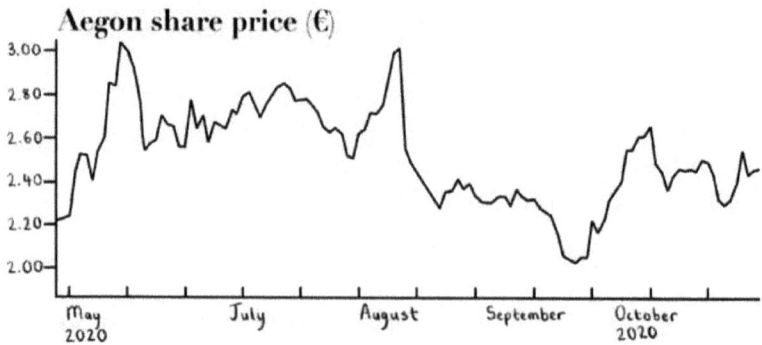

Aegon share price (€)

I got ahead of myself!

I coulda made a handy profit if I had sold in June or July!

Why didn't you stay in bed until June, you blithering idiot?

NN Group

The proceeds of the sale of Unibail Rodamco Westfield part-funded **the purchase of 132 shares at €25.57 in the Dutch insurer NN Group, at an all-in cost of €3,419.**

The Dividend yield for NN Group, at that time, was 7.7%....*wow!*

I continued my love affair with Insurance shares.

Where next?

Canada is a rich country which should ensure a strong economic and stock market performance.

Power Corporation of Canada

Power Corporation of Canada is not a utility. It is a Financial Services Company with a large presence in

Insurance. One of its Insurance subsidiaries trades in dear old Ireland.

The share price was showing a steady upward movement.

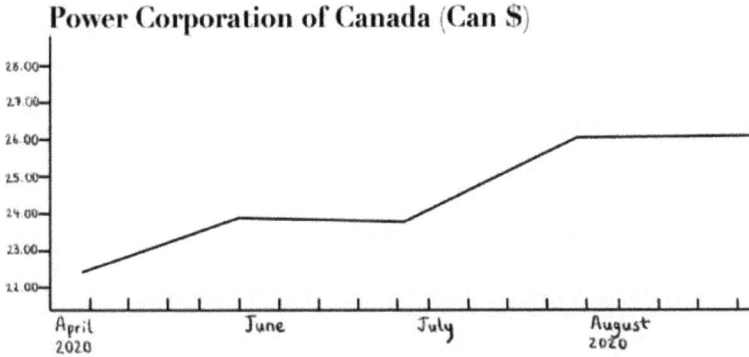

Power Corporation of Canada (Can $)

I decided to buy Power Corporation of Canada shares throughout Summer 2020.

The Vonovia sales (see above) part-funded the purchases of these **Power Corporation of Canada** shares which came with a Dividend yield of c.7%....*nice when you can get it!*

Power Corporation of Canada

Purchase	Quantity	Price	Cost
24/06/2020	185	€23.81	€2,915
12/08/2020	230	€26.97	€4,042
02/09/2020	77	€26.18	€1,351

I changed my €5,000 limit per shareholding upwards to €10,000 to take more advantage of the *'much hoped-for bounce back'* in the market.

I would either be seen as foolish and greedy or brave and clever!

Aviva Insurance

Aviva PLC had decreased their Dividend by 68%+…far too low for my portfolio's targets.

No point in hanging around.

On 07/07/2020, I sold the entire holding realizing losses of -€937.

The -€937 loss incurred at the time of the sale was considerably better than the -€1,821 Unrealized Loss at the time of the Covid crash.

Generali

I decided to add to my shareholding in the Italian Insurer Generali with the proceeds from the sale of the Nordea Bank shares.

The Dividend yield at 3.48% was relatively low, but Generali was highly capitalized and highly regarded in Italy.

On 2 December 21st, 2020, I bought an additional 276 Generali shares at an all-in cost of €3,874. The price paid per share was €13.84.

No more transactions for now.

I find Exhaustion is a useful tool in investment!

Did these transactions pay off?

Let's find out.

Chapter Twenty Two
The Markets Start to Bounce Back

"I asked Santa for a bounce back"

Did Stock Markets begin to bounce back during 2020?

Extraordinary growth took place – look at the Nasdaq:

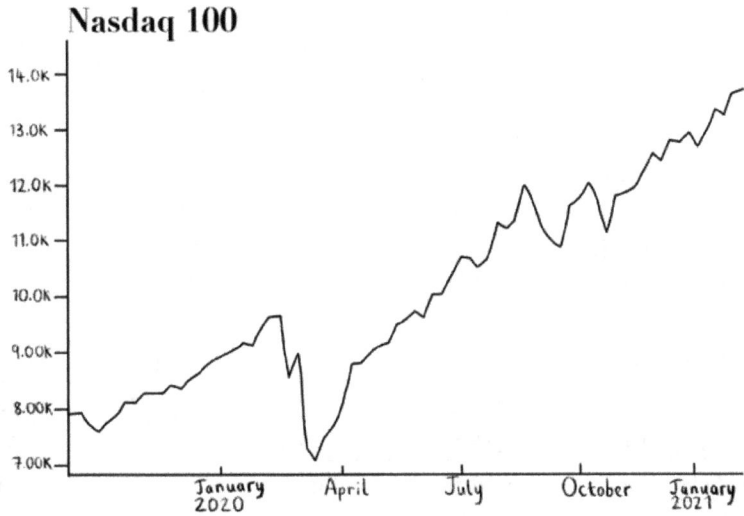

Nasdaq 100

Wow!

We need to factor in the effect on the portfolio of the shares bought and sold in the post-Covid period, April to November 2000, to fully understand the impact of the changing market sentiment on the adjusted portfolio.

Here I present a summary of transactions during the Restructure Period and how the shares performed in the months afterward using December 2020 Valuations as a benchmark.

Hopefully, we can show an improved situation!

Summary of transactions during the Restructure: April to December 2020.

| My Portfolio

Sectors | Mar-20 Portfolio at cost Covid Arrival € | Transactions to December | | December 2020 Portfolio at cost

€ |
		Sales at cost €	Purchases at cost €	
Banks	35,530	-5,355	5,702	35,877
Oil & Basic Resources	22,051	-5,001	14,920	31,970
Autos	12,733			12,733
Pharma	4,603		11,163	15,766
Utilities	19,320		9,742	29,062
UK Retail	4,382	-5,455	1,073	0
Telecoms	8,123	-3,610		4,513
Insurance	50,009	-10,153	23,557	63,413
Large Cap UK Companies	8,386	-9,963	1,577	0
Property & Construction	26,827	-13,964	6,492	19,355
Totals	191,964	-53,501	74,226	212,689

Sales at cost amounted to €53,501, and I spent €74,226 in purchases so, (€74,226 - €53,501) I added in €20,725 net (+11%) in new investment between April 2020 and November 2020, reflecting the view that opportunities presented themselves when markets were trading at all-time lows.

I put in more money when there was blood in the streets!

The March 20 portfolio, therefore, increased, in cost terms, from €191,964 to €212,689 by December 2020.

But what shape was the portfolio in after the restructure?

My Portfolio	December 2020 Portfolio at cost	Portfolio Restructuring Realised Gains/Losses	December 2020 Portfolio Adjusted Costs	December 2020 Portfolio Market Values	December 2020 Portfolio Under/ Over Cost
Sectors	€	€	€	€	€
Banks	35,877	-1,791	37,668	31,730	-5,938
Oil & Resources	31,970	111	31,859	34,785	2,926
Autos	12,733		12,733	15,880	3,147
Pharma	15,766		15,766	17,631	1,865
Utilities	29,062		29,062	33,086	4,024
UK Retail	0	-1,298	1,298	0	-1,298
Telecoms	4,513	-514	5,027	5,479	452
Insurance	63,413	-2,875	66,288	72,667	6,379
Large Cap UK Companies	0	-4,481	4,481	0	-4,481
Property & Construction	19,355	-2,479	21,834	21,082	-752
Totals	212,689	-13,327	226,016	232,340	6,324

Realized Losses and one small gain occurred due to the Restructure:

The -€1,791 loss in the Banks Sector was due to the sale of Nordea Bank, while the exit from Covestro, in **Oil & Basic Resources,** realized **a very small €111 profit.**

Losses occurred in **UK Retail** due to the **sale of Sainsbury's** and in **Telecoms** when **the AT&T holding was exited**.

The **losses in the Insurance Sector** arose from the sales of the holdings in **Aegon and Aviva**.

The losses in the UK Large Cap holdings occurred when the **WPP and Carnival Cruise holdings were sold**.

The small gain from the sale of **Vonovia** was insufficient to make up for the large loss due to the exit from the **Unibail Rodamco Westfield** shareholding and also the smaller loss which occurred when UK Builder, **Barratt Developments**, was sold.

These overall net Portfolio losses of -€13,327 need to be added to the original portfolio cost of €212,689 to arrive at the total acquisition cost of the December 2020 portfolio.

Portfolio valuations needed to reach €226,016 to break even.

By December 2020, the valuation of the portfolio had exceeded breakeven by €6,324

...thank goodness!

Banks, however, continued to report high losses, with all Bank shareholdings showing Unrealized Losses except for **small gains in UBS and Canadian Imperial Bank of Commerce (CIBC)**.

UK Retail, Large Cap, and Property & Construction showed overall losses which arose when exiting these sectors.

All the remaining sectors were now showing profits, and I was hoping for continuing improvements.

Covid-19 was still wreaking havoc around the world, and lockdowns were in force in many countries.

However, the vaccination program was proceeding apace and was beginning to show that it could reduce severe illness.

Would we ever get back to the glory days before the dreaded pandemic had severely hurt stock prices?

It was now a matter of *wait and see...*

Chapter Twenty Three
Back to the Glory Days:
The Post-Covid Valuations

"Thank god that's over"

As Summer 2021 was approaching, the share prices were moving back to the glory days before the pandemic. Many people were now vaccinated and Covid numbers fell. Businesses experienced higher sales as lockdowns were eased. The portfolio survived the Covid storm.

My Portfolio Sectors	May 2021 Portfolio Costs €	May 2021 Portfolio Market Values €	May 2021 Portfolio Unrealized Gains €	Pre-Covid 2020 Portfolio Unrealized Gains €
Banks	37,667	44,673	7,005	417
Oil & Basic Resources	31,860	39,092	7,232	2,922
Autos	12,733	21,900	9,167	4,292
Pharma	15,766	18,679	2,913	3,455
Utilities	29,061	34,679	5,618	7,705
UK Retail	1,298	0	-1,298	20
Telecoms	5,028	5,306	278	3,196
Insurance	66,287	81,322	15,035	14,540
Large Cap UK Companies	4,481	0	-4,481	530
Property & Construction	21,835	22,945	1,110	4,708
Totals	226,016	268,595	42,579	41,785

Stock markets had bounced back. *Hallelujah!*

By May 2021, the portfolio's Unrealized Gains were slightly ahead of those calculated at pre-Covid peak valuations, even after taking into account the cost of the restructuring.

Unrealized Gains totaled €42,579 in May 2021 compared to the figure of €41,785 calculated before the arrival of the virus.

Many investors were betting on the Cyclicals to outperform as economic activity was journeying back to full health.

The improved valuations in Oil & Basic Resources and Autos valuations certainly did not disappoint.

Also, the gains in Banks of €7,005 compared very favorably against their pre-Covid Gains of €417.

Property & Construction failed to recover its pre-Covid highs mainly due to the loss incurred when exiting **Unibail Rodamco Westfield**.

I continue to hold the view that, in the future, shopping malls will find it more difficult as more customers move to online shopping.

The Defensives, **Pharma, and Utilities** had not yet returned to their pre-Covid highs but give these *slow coaches* more time, please!

The **UK Retail and Large Cap Companies** continued with their Realized Losses, which arose when these shares were sold.

The sale of **AT&T** was the reason for the failure of the **Telecoms** holdings to match their pre-Covid highs...*good riddance!*

Could valuations continue to rise from here on in?

At this stage, I was asking myself: was the market frothy? Had I seen the best of the rising share prices?

With the pandemic still ravaging economies, was there a day of reckoning coming down the line?

But then, seven months later, in December 2021, more good news was on the way!

By that December, Unrealized Gains were now €56,761 compared to the figure posted in May 2021 of €42,579.

My Portfolio Sectors	December 2021 Adjusted Costs €	December 2021 Market Values €	December 2021 Unrealized Gains €	May 2021 Unrealized Gains €
Banks	37,667	42,459	4,791	7,005
Oil & Basic Resources	31,860	38,529	6,669	7,232
Autos	12,733	21,948	9,215	9,167
Pharma	15,766	21,517	5,751	2,913
Utilities	29,061	38,375	9,314	5,618
UK Retail	1,298	0	-1,298	-1,298
Telecoms	5,028	5,247	219	278
Insurance	66,287	89,207	22,920	15,035
Large Cap UK Companies	4,481	0	-4,481	-4,481
Property & Construction	21,835	25,495	3,660	1,110
Totals	226,016	282,777	56,761	42,579

December unrealized gains of €56,761 were also comfortably ahead of pre-Covid valuations of €41,785.

Between May 2021 and December 2021, there were small reductions in the **Banks** and **Oil & Basic Resources** Cyclical sectors as investors (not including me) switched to Growth Stocks, as evidenced by the sharp percentage increase in the shares of Apple, up 40% and also Microsoft, up 25%.

However, other investors (including me) switched to Value shares, such as the **Insurance Sector**, attracted by the flow of Dividends,

The **Insurance sector's** Unrealized Gains had increased by a little over 50% in this period. The newly acquired shares in **Power Corporation of Canada** and the **NN Group**, a Dutch Insurer, were major contributors to the improvements in that sector. These shares were bought when there *was blood on the streets*.

The Defensive sectors, **Pharma and Utilities,** also came good during this latest period as investors also flocked into them,

I switched from **Sainsbury's** to **Rio Tinto** during Summer 2020.

The **Rio Tinto share price subsequently rose by 55%,** which more than made up for the loss on the sale of **Sainsbury's.**

I had jumped onto a faster horse!

Overall, the Portfolio's unrealized gains increased by a third.

Happy days!

Then on 22 February 2022, Vladimir Putin decided to invade Ukraine…and the markets went into shock once more!

How did my portfolio, which was already weathering a global pandemic, now cope with the breakout of war?

Chapter Twenty Four
War in Ukraine: A New Challenge

"Grr.. let me at him"

Market shocks

This book describes the impact of two big shocks that impacted financial markets in the period from 2008 to 2022.

The first shock was from the Global Financial Crisis in the United States in 2008, which spread to Europe and other developed economies around the world.

The second shock was the market response to the arrival of the Covid-19 pandemic.

Markets experienced sharp declines followed by gradual recoveries.

The Covid shock was brief, beginning in 2020 and ending in 2021.

The Financial Crisis shock lasted more than twice as long.

The two shocks had different causes.

The Global Financial Crisis shock was a demand shock, and the Covid-19 shock was a supply shock.

Demand shocks, where consumers experience sharp falls in disposable income, lead to increasing unemployment and reduced inflation; Supply shocks, when businesses cannot get an adequate supply of goods, lead to higher prices, leading to increased inflation.

If you decide to become invested in financial markets, you should be prepared to experience shocks.

Remember: It is important not to panic because markets do come back, partly because of appropriate monetary and fiscal policies taken by central banks and governments.

Also, there is the natural resilience of relatively free markets where excess supplies cause prices to fall and excess demand causes prices to rise. Businesses and individuals tend to respond to these price signals in ways that help the economy to recover.

The increased prices encourage more production (when it is needed), and lower prices cause declines in production (when economies are producing too much).

Therefore, as the economy recovers, the stock markets recover.

Ukraine

In 2022, just as we seemed to be putting the Covid-19 shock behind us, Vladimir Putin sent Russian troops into Ukraine to help re-establish the lost Soviet Empire.

Were the markets affected?

But of course……

In the United States:

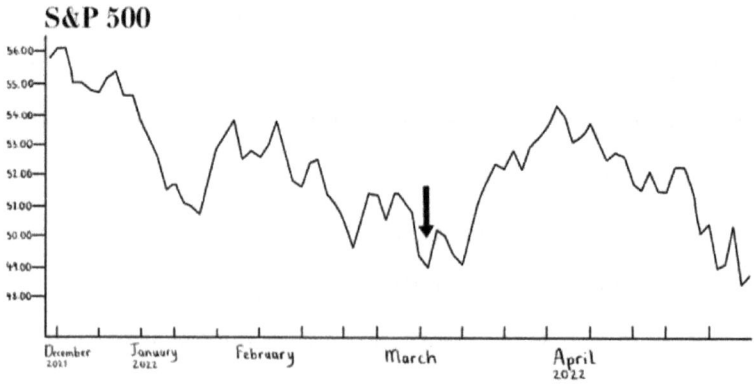

S&P 500

In Germany:

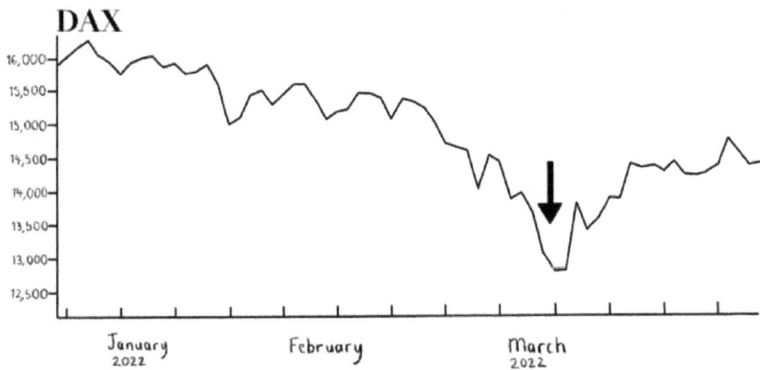

DAX

In the UK:

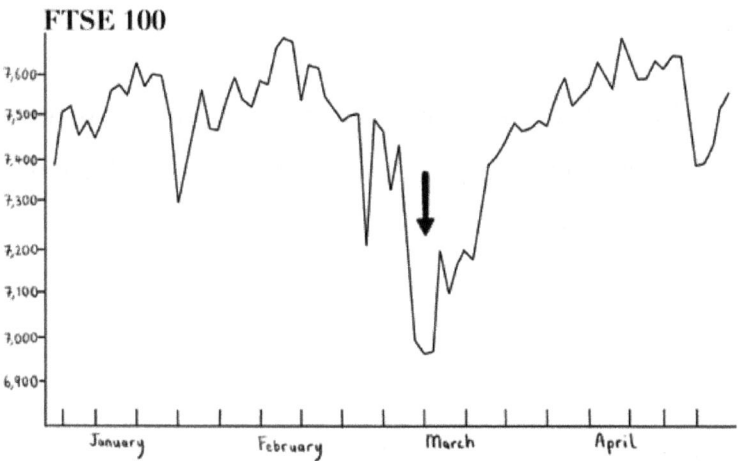

FTSE 100

The impact of the Russian invasion of Ukraine caused sharp share price declines in all major markets, though, within weeks, the markets had returned to previous levels and resumed previous trends.

The US and German markets recovered but then resumed the downward trends that they were experiencing before the war in Ukraine.

It was different in the UK as the London FTSE 100 has a disproportionate number of Energy and Basic Resources companies, e.g., **BP, Shell, Rio Tinto, and BHP Group**.

These shares were stable before the war in Ukraine as they continued to benefit from the economic bounce back, post Covid-19, meaning the overall FTSE 100 share index was in better shape before the war started.

So, in the weeks following the Russian invasion, the London market recovered to its previous level and resumed a more stable trend. This was in contrast to the resumed declines in US and German markets.

How did my portfolio handle the breakout of war? Let's look at the change in the portfolio between December 2021 and April 2022.

My Portfolio	April 2022 Portfolio Adjusted Costs	April 2022 Portfolio Market Values	April 2022 Portfolio Unrealized Gains	December 2021 Portfolio Unrealized Gains
Sectors	€	€	€	€
Banks	37,667	41,207	3,540	4,791
Oil & Basic Resources	31,860	42,812	10,952	6,669
Autos	12,733	20,083	7,350	9,215
Pharma	15,766	24,737	8,971	5,751
Utilities	29,061	41,830	12,769	9,314
UK Retail	1,298	0	-1,298	-1,298
Telecoms	5,028	4,995	-33	219
Insurance	66,287	86,233	19,946	22,920
Large Cap UK Companies	4,481	0	-4,481	-4,481
Property & Construction	21,835	23,242	1,407	3,660
Totals	226,016	285,139	59,123	56,761

Despite the Russian invasion, portfolio valuations *increased* between December 2021 and April 2022, as evidenced by the **increase in Unrealized Gains from €56,761 to €59,123.**

Unbelievable! Yippee!

What happened to the Cyclicals?

Oil & Basic Resources jumped in value. However, **bank shares** declined as the very low interest rate environment continued to depress bank earnings.

*When the good times return, like the phoenix, **bank share prices** will rise from the ashes and return to their former glory!*

What happened to the Defensives?

Pharma and Utilities stocks had a very good run since December 2021.

Let's look at Pharma here:

My Portfolio Pharma	April 2022 Portfolio Adjusted Costs €	April 2022 Portfolio Market Values €	April 2022 Portfolio Unrealized Gains	December 2021 Portfolio Unrealized Gains €
Bayer	11,037	12,895	1,858	-1,375
Pfizer	2,406	6,128	3,722	4,476
Viatris	126	156	30	65
AbbVie	2,197	5,558	3,361	2,585
Totals	15,766	24,737	8,971	5,751

Bayer improved markedly, while **Pfizer** and **AbbVie** canceled out each other's small changes.

Pfizer's offshoot, **Viatris,** declined by a very insignificant amount.

Overall, Pharma delivered a very satisfactory result.

And the Utilities?

There were increases in the valuations of every one of the Utilities.

I am as happy as a dog with two tails!

There was a clear message that investors were moving into Defensives.

That is to be expected if a recession is expected.

Investors switched to Defensives as they would be best able to survive in the bad times.

What were the danger signals that encouraged a more pessimistic outlook at this time?

Inflation

Unprecedented increases in demand for goods and services were being experienced as countries shook off the worst effects of the pandemic.

Supply had not been able to keep up with this demand, and prices were rising sharply.

Central Banks had assumed that these inflationary pressures were transitory, but the continuing war in Ukraine exacerbated conditions, and inflation was now expected to last for a longer time.

The problem with inflation remaining in place over a relatively long period is that workers will demand compensatory increases in wages, and businesses will then push up prices to compensate.

These kinds of 'second round effects' prolong the inflation agony.

All in all, it is a dangerous time for businesses and a bad outlook for share prices.

Governments and Central Banks

During the pandemic, Monetary and Fiscal Authorities worked together to provide extra finance to Governments at very little interest cost.

However, since December 2021, Central Banks began raising interest rates and calling in the substantial funding they had provided to markets. They were beginning to become very worried about inflation.

Higher interest costs, and a squeeze on disposable incomes, will make it difficult for households, companies, and governments to fund their activities, leading to sharply lower economic activity.

This is bad news for stock prices.

Future priorities

I am reminded of the following discourse that I had at the onset of the Financial Crisis in 2009:

A distinguished Bank pensioner approached me and asked me to confirm that our Bank would not be paying a Dividend. I explained to him that it was in the public domain that the bank would report a loss in the billions in the upcoming Financial Results.

"My God," he said, "I don't care what happens to the share price. That is a risk that will be borne by my children when they inherit my portfolio. But I need the Dividend income now to fund my lifestyle."

For those of us who use the stock market to generate extra income, it's about Dividends, Dividends, Dividends.

We can rarely predict large events like major market shocks, so I continually monitor my shares, and I will usually sell if my investment goals are affected.

The reasons for me to sell boil down to the following:

#1 Dividends are cut.

and/or

#2 Share prices are trading at 35%+ from cost, then I cash in the profits.

and/or

#3 Share prices are trading at 35%- below cost, then I get out fast.

and/or

#4 Bad news about the company is published.

and/or

#5, I get fed up with a constant decline in the share price.

Other than in those circumstances, I have learned to be patient, sit tight, hold the line, and stay with the bird in my hand!

Section C

Dealing in Shares: Some Practical Tips

I hope the lessons from my own experiences building a portfolio – Section A - and navigating a pandemic and wartime market shocks - Section B – will help you, the investor, that engages directly in markets.

In the next section of the book - Section C – I hope to arm you with practical tools and tips you will need as you undertake your own investing journey.

Many people are looking for sure fire gains when investing in the stock market. As we have seen, there are no certainties when investing in the markets.

Most investors did not foresee the Financial Crisis, the arrival of the pandemic, or the invasion of Ukraine by Russia.

But my personal journey shows that an ordinary investor can make money from stock market activities even in these times of unprecedented upheaval.

Stock markets bounce back!

We cannot control pandemics, financial disorder, or war, so we must concentrate on dealing in shares using buckets of common sense.

This section of the Book outlines various thoughts and practices that I believe will keep losses to a minimum and generate adequate returns to justify investing.

Chapter Twenty Five
How to Access the Market:
Ways to Get Involved

"Do you want to knock or will I?"

Accessing the market

I will not attempt to answer the question of what the cheapest or best website is when buying and selling shares.

There are many websites available, and it cannot be that a particular website will always be the cheapest or best.

It is best to ask colleagues, friends, or family what websites they are using and choose based on their experiences.

Overseas Companies

Some companies list their stock on more than one stock exchange.

For example, Toyota Motor Corp lists in Tokyo, London, New York, and several other exchanges.

American Depository Receipts (ADRs) (source Investopedia.com)

ADRs offer U.S. investors an effective way to purchase stock in overseas companies that would not otherwise be available.

Foreign firms also benefit, as ADRs enable them to attract American investors and capital without the hassle and expense of listing directly on U.S. stock exchanges.

An American Depositary Receipt is a certificate issued by a U.S. bank that represents shares in foreign stock.

These certificates trade on American stock exchanges.

ADRs and their dividends are priced in U.S. dollars.

ADRs represent an easy, liquid way for U.S. investors to own foreign stocks.

To begin offering ADRs, a U.S. bank must purchase shares on a foreign stock exchange. The bank holds the stock as inventory and issues an ADR for domestic trading. ADRs list on either the New York Stock Exchange (NYSE) or the Nasdaq, but they are also sold over the counter (OTC).

ADR holders do not have to transact the trade in foreign currency or worry about exchanging currency on the forex market. These securities are cleared through U.S. settlement systems.

Sponsored ADRs

A bank issues a sponsored ADR on behalf of the foreign company. The bank and the business enter into a legal arrangement.

The foreign company usually pays the costs of issuing an ADR and retains control over it, while the bank handles the transactions with investors. Sponsored ADRs are categorized by what degree the foreign company complies with Securities and Exchange Commission (SEC) regulations and American accounting procedures.

Unsponsored ADRs

A bank can also issue an unsponsored ADR. However, this certificate has no direct involvement, participation, or even permission from the foreign company.

One primary difference between the two types of ADRs is where they trade. All except the lowest level of sponsored ADRs register with the SEC and trade on major U.S. stock exchanges. Unsponsored ADRs will trade only over the counter. There are 2,000+ ADRs available, which represent companies from more than 70 different countries.

Have you had the time to keep an eye on your shares?

Ask yourself how much support do you want when accessing the market.

 Direct investors need time and expertise to manage their investments.

Many people already live very busy lives or prefer to spend their spare time engaged in leisure activities like sports or the arts.

Their weekends might be devoted, at this stage in their lives, to looking after their children.

If, on the other hand, an investor is retired, working part time, or has a genuine interest in investing in shares, they might be able to squeeze out sufficient time to engage directly in the market.

Dedicating a couple of hours a month would usually be more than adequate to manage your own stock portfolio.

Using third parties to access the markets.

I believe very strongly that investors should use third parties to invest their funds for them unless they can put aside time to deal with their investments each month.

So how should you do this?

Option #1 Using Fund Managers

A 'Fund' is a group of shares that are bundled together – and managed closely by a professional fund manager working at a heavily regulated insurance or fund management company, such as Zurich, Standard Life, or Aviva.

On the advice of a professional fund manager, you select one of their existing funds that best suits your needs and risk appetite.

For example, many investors use a balanced type of fund.

These funds invest a proportion in Bank deposits, shares, bonds, and property.

Other investors might want their funds exclusively devoted to shares.

Investing in a Fund through a professional fund manager means that you gain the benefit of the manager's time, knowledge, and expertise.

The Fund Manager can use a range of techniques to hedge risks for the overall fund, therefore, keeping your investments that bit safer.

The downside to using a professional fund manager is the annual charge for the service.

It is typically more than 1% per year of your investment amount.

In good years, these charges will eat into the Funds' profits. In bad years, these charges are still payable... *oops!*

What kind of returns can I expect from a professionally managed Fund?

No matter what Fund you opt for, there is a risk of losses.

Even experts can get it wrong.

The safest approach is to look at a fund manager's <u>long-term</u> performance.

Anybody can have a lucky year or two, but make sure to find out the Fund's performance over a five- and ten-year timeframe, as this will be much more insightful.

Compare the performances across different Fund Managers and see who performs consistently well.

Option #2 Using Stockbrokers

When using a stockbroker, an investor has three options to choose from:

Execution only – cheapest fees

Stockbrokers will execute the trades, but the decisions on what to buy and sell are decided exclusively by the investor.

Advisory and Execution

The Stockbroker will advise on shares to be purchased and sold. The stockbroker also executes any of these suggestions, subsequently chosen by the investor. Higher fees are charged for this higher level of service, as the investor is supported by recommendations from the Broker.

Discretionary Service (dearest fees/highest level of service)

At this level of service, the Stockbroker is given the discretion and authority to choose investments for the client. They will buy and sell in line with the Client's Suitability Report.

They are legally obliged to understand the risk appetite of the investor.

1. What proportion of the funds should be put into Bonds, equities, or Bank deposits?
2. How much into overseas markets
3. Emerging markets
4. Anything else

For example, I am not comfortable investing long-term in BRICS:

Brazil, Russia., India, China, and South Africa.

Neither do I hold shareholdings in Emerging markets such as Africa, Indonesia, Iran, South Korea, Mexico, Saudi Arabia, Taiwan, and Turkey.

I reckon I can meet my savings objectives via Developed Countries' stocks. I also mostly avoid modern technology stocks and small-cap stocks.

It is, of course, true that from time to time, the shares that I mostly avoid perform exceptionally well.

So be it!

The Financial Regulator regulates brokers to check that regulations are being followed and that brokers understand and abide by their clients' appetite for risk-taking.

Significant fines are imposed on brokers, and they can also lose their licenses if the Financial Regulator loses confidence in their competency or duty of care.

Therefore, investors should feel safe knowing that well-known stockbrokers have a lot to lose if they do not follow regulations.

The level of service they provide, execution only, advisory or discretionary, is up to you.

"You pay your money, and you take your choice."

Option #3 Using an Exchange Traded Fund (ETF)

An Exchange Traded Fund (ETF) is a type of investment that is made up of a large collection of shares.

It is managed by a computer program that uses an algorithm that follows the market's movements and switches in and out of companies according to the changing profile of the chosen market.

For example, if an ETF tracks Banks on the New York stock market, and a new bank is now quoted on that market, the computer program will buy shares in that bank to ensure the ETF exactly represents the market.

An ETF can be made up of any kind of combination of shares.

An investor could purchase an ETF that tracks the performance of all Insurance shares quoted in the FTSE 100.

An ETF can track bonds, oil futures, gold bars, foreign currency, etc.

You can access an ETF using the website that you normally use to buy shares.

The ETF Fund Manager's expertise is not required to choose shares as that function is carried out by the computer program.

The result is that fund management fees are sharply reduced.

Investing in ETFs is a smart way to invest in the markets for those who have little time or interest in tracking individual shares.

ETFs are also less risky than individual stocks as they move in line with the movement in an overall basket of shares, thereby completely avoiding the unique risk attached to one individual share.

ETFs also provide a safer way to invest in Emerging Markets stocks where a lack of familiarity with individual companies makes investments in specific companies often a "plunge in the dark".

An investor does not need to know the intricacies of the accounting regulations used by Chinese companies!

Most ETFs do not capture Dividend income.

However, some are constructed so that the investor is entitled to the earned interest and/or Dividends paid.

Examples of Widely Traded ETFs

One of the most widely known US ETFs tracks the Standard & Poor 500 Index and is called the Spider (SPDR).

The QQQ index tracks the Nasdaq 100, and the DIA index tracks the Dow Jones Industrial Average.

There are ETFs that track individual sectors, such as oil companies (OIH), energy companies (XLE), financial companies (XLF), biotech (BBH), and so on.

Commodity ETFs exist to track commodity prices, including crude oil (USO), gold (GLD), silver (SLV), and natural gas (UNG).

ETFs are increasingly popular:

For the first time ever, annual global net inflows into exchange-traded funds (ETFs) surpassed $1 trillion in 2021, and this milestone was reached in November. This brought total global assets invested in ETFs close to $9.5 trillion, more than twice their value as of the end of 2018, according to data compiled by investment research firm Morningstar Inc.

Decision Time

To decide the best approach for your portfolio, consider how much time and interest in the stock market you personally have.

If you have little time to track the market, you should hand over your funds to one or more Fund Managers.

Nowadays, many investors are instructing Brokers to place their funds in ETFs as they have the cheapest fees.

You always have the option to spread your approach.

I enjoy following the markets, so I use my Stockbroker on an Execution Only basis. I built and managed my own stock portfolio.

That said, to spread the risk, I separately allocated a portion of my funds to be invested professionally in European equities (shares) using a Fund manager who charges a higher level of fees.

I wait, with interest, to see what the 'experts can achieve with that money!

Chapter Twenty Six
The Trader's Toolbox:
Using Technical Indicators

"I have all the tricks of the trade"

What's a Trader?

When people think of the stock market, often the stereotype that comes to mind will be of people creating the frenetic activity usually seen in short-term or day trading.

Traders take the 'pulse' of a share by watching its movements minute by minute and pouncing suddenly, buying or selling, in the belief that their timing is optimal.

Traders work by profiting from <u>short-term price volatility</u> by making trades that last anywhere from several <u>seconds</u> to several weeks.

<u>They buy with the intention of selling and vice versa.</u> Their trades are completed very quickly.

One Trader pointed out to me that his time horizon was not always short, as once, <u>he had held on to a share for a week!</u>

Patterns

Traders use Patterns to buy and sell shares.

They argue that one of the central tenets of the market is that it repeats itself in clear, unmistakable patterns.

Head-and-shoulder patterns, rounding tops and bottoms, ascending and descending triangles, and double and triple tops are proven shapes and patterns that can be identified in stock market graphs.

These patterns are referred to as **Technical Indicators**.

Here I will provide a brief explanation for some easy-to-understand Technical Indicators as they can help time a purchase (or a sale) of a share.

But I would advise readers that wish to get seriously involved in Day Trading to purchase a specialist book that is devoted exclusively to the subject, as I am not a Day Trader.

A trader scrutinizes the charts of shares each day, looking for patterns.

These patterns occur in very short time frames, sometimes over several minutes, or an hour, or sometimes over days.

These patterns inform the trader whether to buy or sell or short sell (sell first and buy later) based on the predicted behavior of the share.

What creates these patterns?

Markets are made up of buyers, whose activities will drive the share price up (optimists), and sellers, whose activities will drive the share price down (pessimists).

This daily activity, when viewed over time, appears to create recognizable repeating patterns in charts/graphs.

Here is an example of a 'Head & Shoulders' chart.

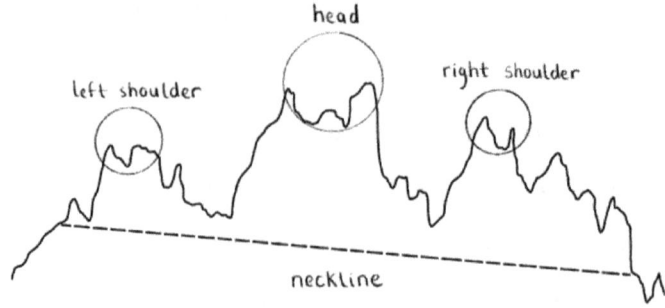

A trader would 'spot' a potential 'head and shoulders' pattern emerging in a share, indicating whether that share is going to fall or rise.

The trader would buy when the share price is at the lower end of "shoulder" and sell when the share price reaches the head and try to repeat this formula again and again.

Here is an example of a 'Support and Resistance' chart:

Support and Resistance occur when a share is trading within a very particular range.

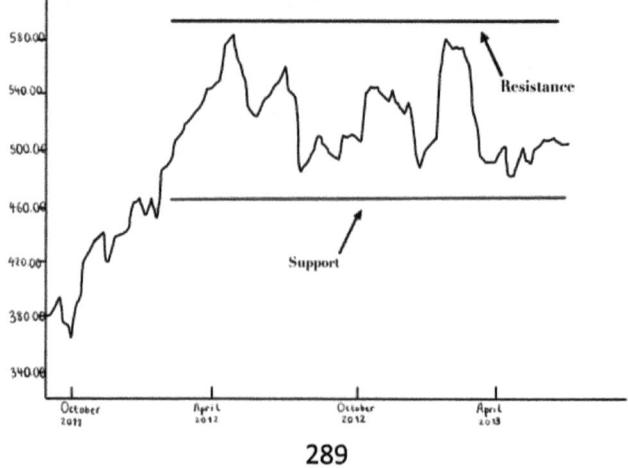

Every time the price goes close to the 'Resistance' line, the share price falls back, and every time it veers near the 'Support' line, it starts to rise.

What this means is that the market stops buying the share when it goes over a certain price – in other words, it 'resists' the price going higher than this point. Similarly, the market seems to 'support' the share price from falling below a certain point. The daily activity in the share price tends to oscillate between these lines.

To make the most profits, a trader would buy when the price was near the Support Line and sell when the price was close to the Resistance Line.

Of course, these chart patterns don't work all the time, but Traders bet that they work 'sufficiently' often to enable profits to be made.

All patterns also come to an end. When this happens, it is called a <u>Technical Breakout</u>.

'History repeats itself, first as a reality, and eventually as a tragedy.

Karl Marx   Misquoted'

The secret to profitable trading is to make sure your losses when a <u>breakout</u> occurs are less than your profits previously made.

"Never trade with all your profits!"

February 11, 2014, Belfast Telegraph

Businessman Sean Quinn was a "fool to believe" in Anglo-Irish Bank investments that cost his family billions of euros in just two years, he has told a court.

He said that in 2007/8, his family lost €3.2bn (£2.6bn) through "the Anglo fiasco".

Undoubtedly, there is money to be made by trading on volatility, but it is very difficult and not for the faint-hearted.

For me, this activity is a Pass!

Make up your own mind...

Savers

Savers, in contrast to Traders, purchase shares in the market with the hope that, <u>over time,</u> share prices will rise.

They hope these rises will be sufficient to pay for their kids' future college education or provide cash to support their future retirement needs etc.

People new to the stock market often try to become Traders to make a quick buck, but after some painful losses, they may move on to become Investors/Savers who buy with a longer-term view for their portfolio.

I buy shares with the aim of saving for the long term. I do not usually trade on a short-term basis.

However, all investors - no matter your time horizon - can benefit by borrowing from a Trader's toolbox when it comes to **the timing** of purchases and sales of a share.

Simple Moving Average

A very useful Technical Indicator is the Simple Moving Average (SMA) – a line that is calculated by looking at the historical share price and averaging this over a period.

The SMA is compared over time to each day's share price.

If the share is below its moving average, it is priced cheaply. If the share is above the SMA, it is considered overpriced. The chart below shows several occasions when a volatile share price dipped below the Simple Moving Average (SMA).

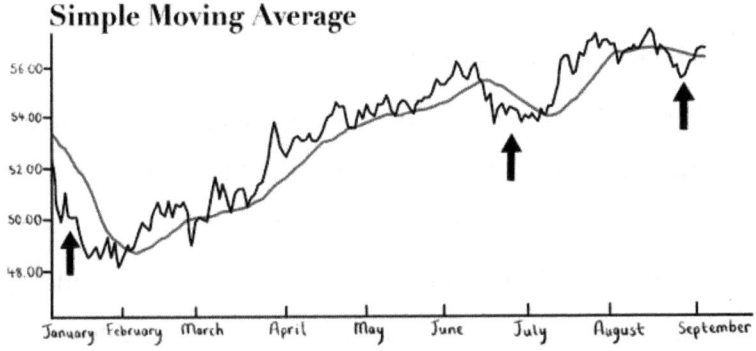

Each time the share price dipped below its SMA, the subsequent move in the share price was upward.

Over time, the share price is expected to return close to its Moving Average.

Therefore, before purchasing any share, you should look at the SMA chart and ask: *Should I buy now or wait for a few days?*

Another useful indicator is the Relative Strength Index (RSI).

Relative Strength Index

The Relative Strength Index (RSI) is a measurement used by Traders to assess the <u>price momentum</u> of a particular stock.

It is a ratio that shows you the number of days that a share finishes <u>above</u> its opening price directly compared to the number of days that the share finishes <u>below</u> its opening price.

The RSI plots this result on a scale of 0 to 100.

If the RSI is high (from 70 - 100), then a lot of traders are buying, and the share price finishes higher at the end of the day than the price at which it opened.

If the RSI is low (from 0 - 30), there is not much bidding activity around this share. Hopefully, future investors will push the share price upwards when they buy 'unloved' (bargain) shares.

What should you do if the RSI is high?

All that buying, which has pushed the RSI higher, will encourage Traders to sell to cash in their profits, and the share price will fall.

Don't buy, and if you already hold the shares, sell.

If the RSI is already low, what this means in practice is the probability is that the "worm will turn" and the share price will go up.

Buy immediately, or if you already hold the shares, don't sell.

Below is a chart that shows how the Walmart share price fell sharply when the RSI was at or above 70 (overbought) in May, August, and December 2022.

Similarly, we can see that the share price rose when the RSI was at or below 30 in May through June 2022.

Towards the end of August 2020, the RSI was trading close to 50 - a neutral position for the price momentum.

Walmart share price (April 2022 to December 2022)

When watching the SMA and the RSI, the message is:

Maximise value by purchasing your chosen shares when the price is <u>below the SMA</u> and the RSI is <u>close to 30</u>.

Borrow from the Wall Street guys and follow the signs!

The next chapter encourages some sensible practices to lower investment losses……hopefully!

Chapter Twenty Seven
Risk Management:
Techniques to Protect Your Money

"Did you mean to test the depth with both feet?"

Understandably, many people are afraid of the uncertainty and risk attached to the stock market.

They worry that they might lose lots of money if they invest in shares.

<u>A key fact about risk is that since most investors are normally risk-averse, markets need to (on average) reward risk-taking.</u>

Otherwise, few investors will take risks!

Risk-taking is key to building wealth.

Speculate to accumulate!

Indeed, it is a key characteristic of entrepreneurs such as Jeff Bezos of Amazon or Elon Musk of Tesla and Space X.

Every day many amateur investors make good money from their portfolios both in terms of capital gains and Dividend income.

What is more important is that mistakes are kept to a minimum.

Here are several well-known risk management techniques that will provide a safety net as you undertake your investment endeavors.

RISK PROTECTION TECHNIQUE #1

Limit on a holding

You should limit the size of each holding, e.g., €5,000 or €10,000.

This spreads your risk, and if any one of your holdings 'tanks', you won't lose everything.

In practice, this means buying 2 or 4 stocks for €20,000 rather than investing the full amount in one stock.

Some stocks will fall, but others will rise.

You lose this protection if you put everything into one stock.

As Warren Buffet famously says: "Never test the depth of the river with both feet".

RISK PROTECTION TECHNIQUE #2

Diversify your portfolio!

Spreading risk across a range of sectors and a mix of Defensive and Cyclical shares will lend a natural resilience to your portfolio.

The following Table from Davy Stockbrokers shows how a diversified portfolio would have minimized losses from the Financial Crash of 2008 if bought at the 'peak' of the Precrash market on 23/2/2007.

1	Bank of Ireland	-92.5%	(-92.5%)
2	Bank of Ireland	-92.5%	(-68.2%)
	Ryanair	-43.9%	
3	Bank of Ireland	-92.5%	(-35.1%)
	Ryanair	-43.9%	
	Paddy Power	31.0%	
4	Bank of Ireland	-92.5%	(-25.2%)
	Ryanair	-43.9%	
	Paddy Power	31.0%	
	Kerry	4.6%	
5	Bank of Ireland	-92.5%	(+7.5%)
	Ryanair	-43.9%	
	Paddy Power	31.0%	
	Kerry	4.6%	
	Apple	124.9%	
	Google	13.0%	
	Gold	56.0%	

In Scenario 1, above, the portfolio would have lost 92.5% at the market low point in 2009 if the portfolio contained only Bank of Ireland shares.

On the other hand, in Scenario 5, if an investor held a diversified portfolio, they would have earned profits of 7.5% in that same timeframe.

Quite the difference!

Limiting the size of each holding naturally facilitates the diversification of your Portfolio, so the two techniques are complementary.

RISK PROTECTION TECHNIQUE #3

Operating a Stop Loss limit

"Knowing when to fold your tent."

Bear in mind the price at which you bought the share.

If the price goes up or down by 10%, that can be considered normal.

If the price rises/falls by 20% from your cost price, put the share 'on watch'.

If a share has risen or fallen by 35%+ from cost price, you should seriously consider acting.

If a share has risen by 35%, you need to ask yourself:

Is this share likely to go up another 35% (70% in total)?

or

Is now the perfect time to cash in and realize your gains?

If a share has risen by 35%, you must question how much farther the share price is likely to go. Sophisticated investors might buy a hedge in the market to limit their downside. But if the amount invested is small, say €5,000 or €10,000, I would be inclined to sell some and cash in my profits.

Similarly, if a share has fallen by 35%, you should seriously question why this has happened.

If the market has pushed the share price down, there is usually a good reason why there is a loss of confidence in the future of this share.

If a share has fallen 35% (especially if the stock market is doing well in the same period), it is unlikely to recover fully for the next few years.

A better decision would be to stem the bleeding, **sell the share, accept the losses, and switch to a share with a brighter future.**

If you want to win the race, get off the slow horse and jump onto the fast horse.

RISK PROTECTION TECHNIQUE #4

Investing in Low Beta Stocks

Every investor sometimes needs to sell some shares to access finance.

For example, they may need to fund a wedding, buy a house, or access money in retirement.

The risk with the stock market is that when you need to sell shares, they are trading at all-time lows.

Happily, you can mitigate this risk by ensuring you are invested in shares that are less volatile than others.

We can identify these using a metric called *Beta*.

Beta measures the volatility of a share.

If a share's Beta is over 1, it is considered more volatile than other shares in the market.

If a share's Beta is less than 1, it is considered less volatile than the market.

Ask Google to tell you a share's Beta.

For example, in September 2021, **Walmart's Beta was 0.4798**.

This is a low Beta, and it means that if the market moves down by 10%, then Walmart is likely to fall by just 4.7% in the same timeframe.

On the other hand, as of September 2021, **Ford had a Beta of 1.1271** which means if the market moves down by 10%, Ford's share price is likely to fall by 12.71% in the same period.

It also means that a Ford share is almost three times more volatile than Walmart's.

That's most likely because buying grocery items is a constant day-to-day spending (Defensive stock), but sales of cars go up and down depending on the economic cycle (Cyclical stock).

Households (and Businesses) postpone big purchases in tough times.

Keeping an eye on a share's Beta gives you a sense of how sensitive these shares will be to any changes in the market, which is important to know if you suddenly need to access your money.

RISK PROTECTION TECHNIQUE #5

Time Horizons

Major global events can have a negative impact on the market, but as we have seen, markets tend to bounce back.

Dips in share prices do not last forever, and the longer you hold a share, the more likely it is that when you come to sell it, the share price will be higher than what you paid for it.

The argument to hold shares for long periods of time is compelling.

If, between 1926 and 2017, investors held shares for one year, they would have had a **one in four** chance that they would lose money selling that share.

If, on the other hand, the investor held the shares for five years, they would only have had a **one in seven** chance of losing money when they came to sell.

If they held the same shares for ten years, the likelihood of the share price being lower than the cost dropped to **one in seventeen**.

There is usually a gentle increase - over time in share prices because companies get an injection from undistributed profits made each year, allowing them to expand and grow over time.

Hold on to your shares, and things will come right.

You don't have to take my word for it.

The following chart plots the inexorable rise in stock prices.

(Source: Macrotrends)

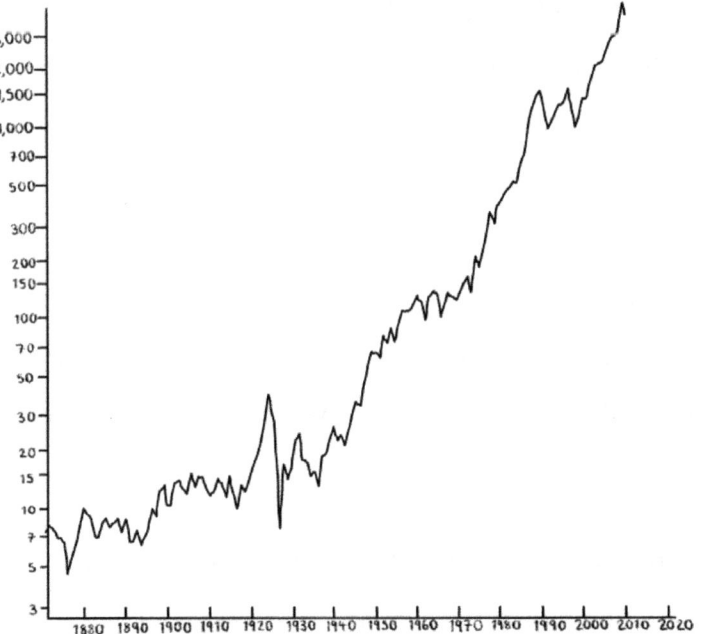

Chart the S&P from 1880 to 2020:

Time is worth waiting for!

Just ask Warren Buffet. His stated time horizon is typical: "forever".

It goes without saying, but...

Don't be in a position where you need to sell at the wrong time.

Every investor should have a cash buffer/bank deposits/borrowings to dip into if they need money while waiting for a depressed market to recover.

RISK PROTECTION TECHNIQUE #6

Selling at the right time

There is a famous saying in the stock market: *"Any fool can buy, but it takes a real genius to know when to sell"*.

Understandably, for investors, if a share price is climbing, the temptation is to hold on and enjoy the ever-increasing paper profits.

Similarly, if the share price is falling, the investor finds it difficult to sell as such an act will crystallize any losses.

But there are occasions when a share should be sold.

How often does the Stock Market lose money?

Negative stock market returns occur, on average, in about one out of every three/four years. However, historical data shows that the positive years far outweigh the negative years.

Markets will rise and fall.

If the majority of shares in the market, including the shares owned by the investor, are declining, then that is a market movement.

General Market movements usually reverse over time.

Some have argued that investors are too scared of recession and overreact.

According to the highly respected economist Paul Samuelson, "the stock market has predicted <u>nine</u> out of the last <u>five</u> recessions".

As an example, investors got spooked and drove the S&P 500 down by 14.82% just coming up to Christmas 2018:

Panicking at the sight of this drop would have been a mistake, as the market recovered within three months.

S&P 500 Index

Hold on to your britches till the market turns!

So, when should an Investor sell?

The main thing to look at is what the <u>individual share price</u> is doing compared to the <u>overall market</u>.

Share prices will rise and fall when the overall market moves.

Just look at how the Ford Motor share price mirrors the S&P 500. Though the graphs are not identical, you can see how the Ford Motor share price, and the overall S&P 500 index, both took a significant dip in July 2019.

The Ford Motor Company declined by 20% between the first week in June 2022 and 26th July 2022.

It had recovered by the end of July 2022. Now if you look at the market (S&P 500) that Ford is listed on:

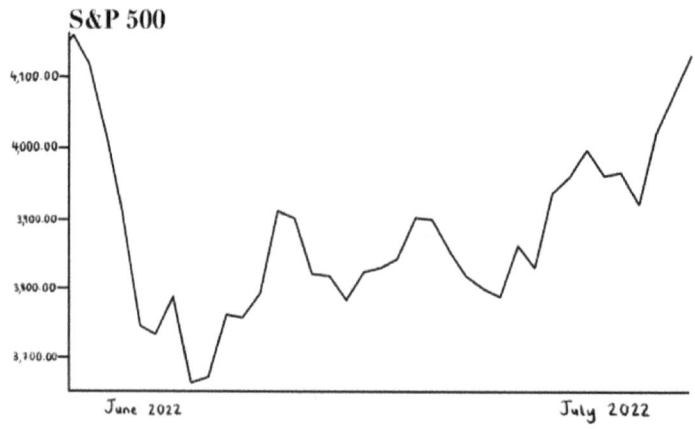

The S&P 500 also declined in the same period.

Importantly, it had also recovered by the end of July 2022.

So, the decline in the share price of Ford Motor reflected the general malaise being felt by market participants.

No need to panic! The market is always moving up and down!

Market declines of 10% are referred to as market 'corrections', which means the markets have run away from reality and need to be clipped back.

If markets decline by 20%, then these movements are described as "Bear markets" because Bears fight by retreating from the enemy (selling shares).

Bears are now in control!

Market rises of 20%, are termed "Bull markets" as bulls rush towards the enemy (buying shares).

Bull and Bear markets (or rises and falls of 20%) are 'par for the course' and are to be expected.

However, if a share price is moving **in the opposite direction** to the movement in its market, there is a problem.

Here is an example of a share price diverging from its market. You can see that BT Group PLC is on a significant downward trend from July 2016, when the FTSE 100 index was on a gentle upward rise.

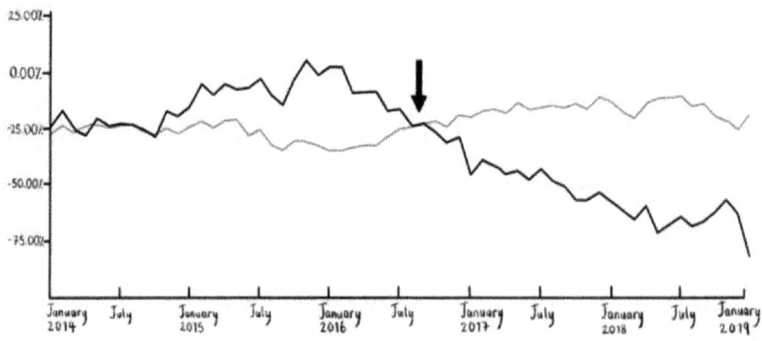

BT Group PLC FTSE 100

Why, oh why, did I not sell in July 2016?

My three takeaways for the strongest sell signals are:

#1 The 35% rule

When the BT share price dipped 35% lower, a trend not shared by movements in the FTSE100 in the same period, alarm bells were pealing.

Don't hang about……sell, sell, sell.

Here is a good example of the benefit of selling when the share price moves <u>up</u> by 35%

The **Netflix** share rose +39%. From January 2018 to $391.43 on 14th June 2018.

If you had held on to the share until then, you would have looked very good, but then the wheels came off.

The share fell to $334.96 towards the end of June.

Don't be greedy! Sell when the share has risen by 35% and pocket the gains!

#2 The second 'sell' signal is a Dividend cut.

A Dividend cut signals that a share is about to enter 'choppy waters'.

Take Disney:

In 2020, Disney suspended its Dividend. Investors did not receive a Dividend in July 2020 and would not get a cash pay-out in January 2021 either.

The board of directors attributed its decision to "the ongoing impact of Covid-19 and the company's decision to prioritize investment in its direct-to-consumer initiatives" (i.e., expansion of the new streaming service Disney+)

Covid-19 had forced Disney to close theme parks and movie theatres.

The Q1 and Q2 2022 results showed that Disney had moved back into profit. But Dividends had still not resumed as the company prioritized investment in Disney+.

A Dividend cut usually highlights that the company's sustainable free cash flow has shrunk very considerably.

As a Dividend investor, I usually exit company shares when their Dividends are cut.

Cash is king!

#3 The third 'sell' signal is if you can generate more money from Dividends elsewhere.

For example, you may have a share where the price has doubled, but the Dividend has not been increased.

This is a ripe opportunity to cash in your profit from the rise in the share price and put the newly generated cash into a new share with a higher Dividend yield.

Doing this means you have kept your original holding (and its Dividend) and now used the profits to buy another share (and a new Dividend stream).

I use these three 'sell signals' to try and exit shares at the right time, but knowing when to sell is definitely an art.

As with all things in life...sometimes I am right, and sometimes I am wrong.

"Sometimes you're the pigeon. Sometimes you're the statue."

The next and final Chapter will give you a 10-step checklist for you to use when deciding if you want to buy a share.

Chapter Twenty Eight
How to Pick a Share:
A Simple 10-Step Checklist

"They all look so good"

I am reminded of the story about the men that lived in a boarding house in Ennis, a small county town in the Midwest of Ireland, in the 1930s. Each Monday morning, at breakfast, one of the men used to regale the others on his fantastic successes at the weekend, attending the horse racing in the neighboring city of Limerick. One day one of the other men gave his savings to the "gambling expert" and asked him to bet them on his behalf. The following Monday, the "expert" again kept his colleagues in awe as he recounted his successes in Limerick that weekend. When asked for an update, on his stake, by the guy who had entrusted his savings to him, the gambler advised: "Very sorry, but your bets all went sour".

Don't rely on "fellahs" to tell you where to invest your hard-earned cash!

Do your own research and check the fundamentals of any company using the following 10 key steps to assessing the health of any share.

Much information can be found in the **Investor Relations section** of a company's website, where the company presents its annual results to its shareholders in the form of a presentation.

Be careful not to take everything at face value, remembering to sanity check the claims made by any company.

"They would say that, wouldn't they?"

Mandy Rice-Davies (misquoted) London, 1960s.

You can also ask **Google.**

We will now go through the 10 steps to assessing any share's potential value:

STEP 1: The Company

Is this a reputable and strong performer in its particular market?

A company that is well known (e.g., **Coca Cola**) that has the longevity, muscle, and scale, will find it easier to generate sales and profits in its market than its smaller competitors.

STEP 2: What is the company planning for the future?

The importance of what the company is planning for the years ahead cannot be overstated, as this will directly impact the current and future price of the share.

Here you should look at what the management is proposing as the company's strategy:

For example, expansion into a new market or diversifying their product line. Does it sound good to you? Are other companies already doing this? Have they a track record of successfully managing CHANGE?

For example, Volkswagen's strategy:

"The world of mobility will change fundamentally by 2030. Electric drive and fully networked transportation with autonomous drive will determine how we move around in the future.

The Volkswagen Group will be a significant driver of this transformation and accelerate its realignment from a vehicle manufacturer to a leading, global software-driven mobility provider.

Their guiding principle is the development of sustainable, connected, safe, and tailored mobility solutions for future generations."

(VW Investor Relations)

The right approach…surely.

Make sure you agree with their approach.

Remember: You invest in the company's future, not its past!

STEP #3: Is Sales Revenue growing?

In other words, is the company holding its position in the market?

DIAGEO

Investor relations;

Net sales	2021	2020
	£12,733m	£11,752m
Reported movement	8.30%	
(Includes currency impacts and acquisitions/ divestments)		
Organic movement	16.00%	
(Compares like with like)		

(I would, personally, have helped them to reach their sales targets for Guinness!)

STEP #4: Is the company making money?

This can be worded in different ways on balance sheets, but what you are looking for is the profits <u>after</u> operating costs and taxes are deducted.

This is sometimes called "net income attributable to shareholders".

These profits will show the money available for reinvestment and Dividends.

Investor relations

Tesco ($BNs)	2022	2021	2020	2019
Annual Income after taxes	2.089	0.934	1.195	1.741

In 2022 income is higher than before the Virus. *Good results by Jove!*

Some emerging companies operate at a loss while they ramp up.

You might still wish to invest in these growing companies if you truly believe in their future.

Never say never! But a risky bet!

 # STEP 5: Has the company too much debt?

Debt-to-EBITDA is a ratio that measures a company's ability to pay off its debt.

Rating Agencies such as Standards & Poor, Moody's, and Fitch Group use this metric to look at a company's debt repayments, much like a bank will check to make sure a customer can afford his mortgage debt repayments.

EBITDA is a measure of a company's cash generation, and its level determines the amount of repayment capacity available to pay off its Borrowings.

Rating Agencies are comfortable if Debt to EBITDA is less than 3.

You can google this ratio for any company.

DIAGEO

In February 2022, **Diageo's net debt was 2.7 times its EBITDA**, which is a significant but still reasonable amount of leverage.

 # STEP 6: Is the company in good hands?

The **Return on Average Invested Capital (ROIC)** is a widely used metric to judge management efficiency in a company.

Some commentators refer to this metric as the **Return on Equity (ROE)**

If ROIC beats 10%, then management has added value to the franchise and delivered acceptable results.

This metric is widely available. All you need to do is google ROIC or ROE and the name of an individual company.

DIAGEO

Diageo's ROE was 52.64% as of December 2021.

An after-tax return for shareholders of over 50%

Wow!

STEP 7: Is the share price trading at attractive levels?

When the P/E Ratio of a company is higher than the average in the market in which it operates, it is expensive.

If a company's P/E Ratio is below the market average, the shares are considered relatively cheap.

Check what index your company is primarily listed on (e.g., FTSE, Nikkei, DAX, etc.) and compare the company's current P/E Ratio to the P/E Ratio of that market.

This will give you a sense of how the share is currently priced.

TESCO PLC

Tesco's P/E Ratio was 12.70 on May 6, 2022

For the FTSE 100, the trailing twelve-month P/E is currently 14.86.

Tesco is cheaper than the market average.

Goodee!

Dividend Yield (google)

Also, look at the Dividend yield, which compares the Dividend paid compared to the current market price of the company's share.

On the same date, May 6 2022, the **Tesco Dividend Yield was 4.30%**

Satisfactory but not top drawer

#STEP 8. Is the Dividend sustainable?

Most companies pay out less than 50% of their profits by way of Dividends, i.e., their Pay-out ratio is less than 50%

TESCO PLC

Current: **Tesco currently has paid out 45% of profits**...*Excellent!*

STEP 9. What do the Financial Analysts think?

Many well-respected international analysts publish projections on a company's share price, and it can be very useful to add these expert views 'into the mix'.

Based on their own assessments, Analysts will usually advocate a Buy, Hold, or Sell strategy for any share.

Google put me straight through to the Diageo investor center:

Diageo showed the Analysts' consensus opinions, together with minimum and maximum opinions for 2022 and 2023.

The story is very exciting for 2022 but just satisfactory in 2023:

	Consensus	Min	Max
F22 FY			
Organic net sales growth (%)	17.1	14.8	18.7
Organic operating profit growth(%)	21.9	19.3	25.4
Organic operating margin expansion (bps)	121	67	167
EPS pre exceptionals & disc ops (p)	142.1	137.3	147.6
Free cash flow (£m)	2,412	1,599	2,985
F23 FY			
Organic net sales growth (%)	6.6	4.3	9.8
Organic operating profit growth (%)	8.0	4.7	11.3
Organic Operating margin expansion (bps)	40	-22	93
EPS pre exceptionals & disc ops (p)	158.4	146.5	167.5
Free cash flow (£m)	3,063	2,593	3,478

STEP 10. Buy when the share price is expected to increase in value.

Borrow from the Traders' toolbox and check the current price against its SMA and its RSI.

If the RSI is 45 or lower, it's a buy signal.

If the RSI is 65 or higher, it is a sell signal.

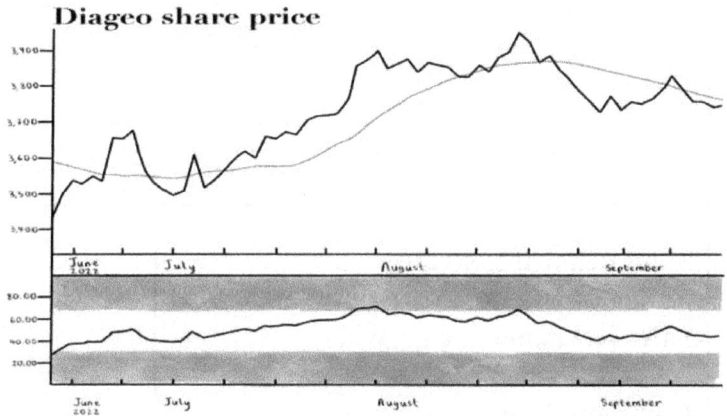

Diageo share price

In early July 2022, the Diageo share was trading mostly below its SMA, and its RSI was in "oversold" territory. These signs send a clear signal to buy.

In August, the share price was trading above its SMA and was in "overbought" territory. A sale around that time would have paid off handsomely!

Checklist to use when picking shares.

Below I have provided a simple 10-step checklist that lists many of the items that I consider when deciding whether to buy a share or not.

The list is neither exhaustive nor mandatory, but I hope it will be useful for you.

It is unlikely that, when evaluating a share, you will be able to place a Y (for Yes) in each box.

However, it should give you pause for thought to see what boxes contain an N (for No).

You will then make a more informed decision.

Checklist

	Tests	Tick Y or N
1	Significant presence in the prospering industry	
2	Solid believable strategy	
3	Sales Revenues are growing	
4	Company is making money	
5	Debt/EBITDA is under 3	
6	Company is in good hands (ROIC/ROE is 10%+)	
7	Current price not expensive (P/E Ratio < 13)	
8	Dividend Yield good (3.5%- 6.5%) and Dividends are sustainable (Pay-out ratio not more than 50% of profits)	
9	Analysts are advocating a 'buy'	
10	Technical Signals strong (price under the SMA and the RSI is 30 - 45)	

Use the Checklist as a starting point when looking for shares to buy.

Buy a few different shares and slowly add to your portfolio.

Slowly, slowly, catchee monkey!

Watch your holdings for sell signals and sell when advisable.

323

Protect your money using my risk management techniques outlined in the previous chapter.

Don't forget that when markets are down, there may be some bargains to be had.

What does a miser do every night before he goes to bed?

He counts his cash... Yes... Yes... Yes!

ENJOY!

Glossary of Terms

(Many explanations sourced from Investopedia.com)

- **ADR**

ADRs represent an easy, liquid way for U.S. investors to own foreign stocks.

Foreign firms also benefit, as ADRs enable them to attract American investors and capital without the hassle and expense of listing directly on U.S. stock exchanges.

An American Depositary Receipt is a certificate issued by a U.S. bank that represents shares in foreign stock. To begin offering ADRs, a U.S. bank must purchase shares on a foreign stock exchange. The bank holds the stock as inventory and issues an ADR for domestic trading.

ADRs list on either the New York Stock Exchange (NYSE) or the Nasdaq, but they are also sold over the counter (OTC).

ADRs and their dividends are priced in U.S. dollars.

- **Averaging down**

Averaging down is an investing strategy that involves a stock owner purchasing additional shares of a previously initiated investment after the price has dropped. The result of this second purchase is a decrease in the average price at which the investor purchased the stock.

- **BETA**

Beta measures the volatility of a share price.

If a share's Beta is over 1, it is considered more volatile than other shares in the market.

If a share's Beta is less than 1, it is considered less volatile than the market.

- **Cyclical Stocks**

Cyclical stocks involve companies that sell items that consumers buy more of during a booming economy but spend less on during a recession. For example, people buy more cars when economies are growing strongly.

- **DAX (30)**

The DAX 30 represents the shares quoted on the Frankfurt (German)stock market.

For example, the Dax 30 covers the 30 largest German shares quoted on the Frankfurt stock market.

- **Defensive Stocks**

Defensive stocks belong to companies that make or sell items that consumers need to buy regardless of the state of the economy. For example, shares in companies that operate in the groceries, medication, and utilities sectors.

- **Demand shocks**

Demand shocks occur when consumers experience sharp falls in disposable income, leading to increasing unemployment and reduced price inflation;

- **Dividend**

A Dividend is a portion of the profits that companies pay out to their shareholders (quarterly, half-yearly, or annually).

It is a cash amount deposited into your account by a company for simply owning a share of their business. It is used by the company as a reward for new investors and to entice existing investors to stick around.

- **Dividend Yield**

The Dividend Yield is a % ratio that shows how much a company pays out in Dividends each year compared to its share price.

The Dividend Yield can be likened to the Interest rate you would receive from the Bank on your deposits.

- **Dividend Stocks**

Dividend stocks will often appeal to Investors and will usually pay good Dividends to attract investors.

- **EBITDA**

EBITDA is a measure of a company's cash generation, and its level determines the amount of repayment capacity available to pay off its Borrowings. It stands for earnings before interest, taxes, depreciation, and amortization.

- **Economic Cycle**

In good times, people buy more, and prices rise. Then items become too expensive, and people buy less. Prices fall, and the economy contracts. The lower prices eventually tempt buyers back into the market, and prices start to rise again, and the economy resumes growth.

And so on...

- **ETF**

An Exchange Traded Fund (ETF) is a type of investment that is made up of a large collection of shares.

It is managed by a computer program that uses an algorithm that follows the market's movements and switches in and out of companies according to the changing profile of the chosen market.

- **FTSE Index**

The FTSE 100 index follows the fortunes of the 100 largest companies on the London Stock Exchange. There are also FTSE 250 and FTSE 500 indices.

- **Growth Stocks**

Growth stocks have substantially higher growth rates than the market average.

But they usually pay out very little by way of Dividends, if anything at all.

Growth companies invest their profits back into the company to fuel further growth.

- **Head & Shoulders share patterns/charts**

A 'head and shoulders' pattern emerging in a share price indicates whether that share price is going to fall or rise. An investor would buy when the share price is at the lower end of the"left shoulder" (price bottom) and sell when the share price reaches the "head" (price top).

The price again falls to the Bottom (the lower end of the right shoulder).

The share price continues to trade in the range between the bottom of the shoulders and the top of the head

- **Large Cap Company**

Market Capitalisation is a measure of company size calculated by multiplying the number of shares issued by a company by the market price of one share.

Large Cap companies are defined by the size of the stock market. Most investors will be familiar with large cap companies as they are the biggest companies in the stock market.

Bigger companies have very diversified operations, and usually, they can survive misfortune more easily. They operate many different products in many different markets.

- **Nikkei Index (Tokyo)**

The Nikkei Stock Index, the Nikkei 225, is used around the globe as the premier index of Japanese stocks.

- **Pay-out Ratio**

The "Pay-out ratio" is the % of profits paid out to shareholders in Dividends each year.

- **Price Earnings Ratio (P/E)**

The price-to-earnings ratio measures a share's current price relative to its earnings per share (EPS)."

If the share price is $100 and the earnings attributable to each share is $10, then the P/E Ratio is 10 times.

- **Price to Book Ratio (P/B)**

The P/B is a ratio used to compare a share's current value to its 'book' value.

It can also be described as the ratio of the market value of a company's shares (share price) over the book value of each share. The book value of each share is the Net Assets of the company divided by the number of its issued shares.

- **Relative Strength Index (RSI)**

The RSI is a ratio that shows you the number of days that a share finishes above its opening price directly compared to the number of days that the share finishes below its opening price.

The RSI plots this result on a scale of 0 to 100.

- **Rights Issue Entitlement**

A 'rights' entitlement is when large discounts are offered by a company to existing shareholders to entice them to buy new shares.

- **ROIC/ROE**

Return on equity (ROE) is a measure of financial performance calculated by dividing net income by shareholders' equity. Because shareholders' equity is equal to a company's assets minus its debt, ROE is considered the return on net assets.

ROE is also called Return on invested capital (ROIC)

- **S&P Index (New York)**

The S&P 100 index follows the fortunes of the 100 largest companies on the US Stock Market. There are also S&P 500 and S&P 1500 indices.

- **Scrip Dividend**

  Instead of receiving a Dividend in cash, additional company shares are issued to shareholders worth the value of the Dividend.

  Scrip Dividends are exempt from stamp duty and dealing charges, which makes their acquisition worthwhile for the investor. Also, the company holds on to the cash it would have paid out in a cash Dividend, so they are an attractive option for companies as well as investors.

- **Share**

  Shares are units of ownership of a company, usually traded on the stock market. They are also known as stocks or equities.

- **Simple Moving Average (SMA)**

  The Simple Moving Average (SMA) is a line that is calculated by averaging the historical share price each day over a specified period.

- **Small Cap Company**

  Market Capitalisation is a measure of company size calculated by multiplying the number of shares issued by a company by the market price of one share.

  Small Cap Companies comprise the smaller companies in each market.

They can be very sensitive to movements in local conditions.

Small companies have the capacity to grow sharply, thereby increasing the share price rapidly…but they can also collapse more quickly!

- **Stop Loss Limit**

Stop-loss orders execute a market order when triggered, and execution of the contract is guaranteed when the stop-loss price is met. Stop-limit orders execute a limit order when the initial stop-loss order is triggered, providing investors more control over the execution price.

- **Support & Resistance share patterns/charts**

Support occurs when a downtrend in a share price is expected to pause.

Resistance occurs when an uptrend in a share price is expected to pause.

Share prices frequently tend to operate in a range between the Support and Resistance levels.

- **Supply Shocks**

Supply shocks occur when businesses cannot get an adequate supply of goods

The shocks lead to higher prices/increased inflation.

- **Technical Breakout**

Chart patterns don't work all the time, but Traders bet that they work 'sufficiently' often to enable profits to be made.

All patterns come to an "unexpected end."

When this happens, it is called a Technical Breakout.

- **Technical Indicators**

Technical indicators are pattern-based signals produced by the price, volume, and/or open interest of a share.

- **Value Stocks**

A Value Stock is a share that the market is pricing incorrectly against its intrinsic value and that the price will increase as the intrinsic value is realized. They are shares that are trading at bargain prices.

Index

Milton Keynes UK
Ingram Content Group UK Ltd.
UKHW020650170824
447045UK00012B/912